Adult Dog Training Through Positive Reinforcement

Learn the Essential Skills Needed to Shape an Obedient and Well-Behaved Dog

Hope Chambers

Table of Contents

Introduction

Picture this, you head to your local shelter, and you lock eyes with your soulmate. A large, furry, mixed breed named Sam. His tail wags and your heart is stolen. You take him home and get ready for the perfect life together, except he is anything but well-behaved.

You have heard that crate training is the best method, but he whines the entire time. The guilt takes over, so you let him out and give him free rein of the house. Suddenly, he has taken your bed, hogged the couch, and chewed up your favorite shoes!

You assumed that he would be housebroken. It's just common sense, right? However, Sam has never lived in a home situation and has taken a liking to your favorite rug as a toilet. He thinks he is being polite, only soiling one spot in the house. The solution? Walking! He will surely learn to potty outdoors then, and exercise is so important to ensure your pup is happy and healthy.

You have already picked out the perfect collar and leash. They were highly recommended by the local pet store. "These are the best on the market, guaranteed no pulling!" they said, but Sam doesn't seem to care. The excitement takes over, and he begins to drag you across the street. You are starting to panic. There are so many dangers around, and he doesn't seem to be aware of them. You immediately drag him back into the house.

The frustration begins to set in, but you try to remain calm and think. Maybe the park is quieter and less overwhelming. He may even meet a friend. You now know that he gets overly excited, but you have a plan! As soon as you pull up to the park, you secure his leash and command him to sit and wait. His tail is wagging, beating against the seat. With his tongue out and eyes wide, he actually sits! You slowly open the door.

In a split second, the sounds and smells of an exciting new world hit him, and what's that? Another dog? He's off! You realize right away this was a mistake. He is just not ready.

Exhausted and overwhelmed, you invite over Aunt Betty. She loves dogs. Perhaps she can convince you that you haven't made a mistake. As she enters your home, 80 pounds of furry, slobbery dog comes bounding up, and with one big jump, Aunt Betty is against the wall. Sam is convinced that these lovely licks and kisses are the only real way to say hello.

You have had enough. Being nice isn't working, and you start to yell, "Get down! Stop it! Bad Dog!!" The worst thought begins to flood your mind: *Should I take him back?*

These are just some examples of the challenges you may face when adopting an untrained adult dog. However, it is so important to take a deep breath and put yourself in their paws. Some dogs have not had the privilege of having an owner who is patient and kind and who followed through with their training. Some dogs have not had the privilege of having an owner at all. Sadly, some dogs have gone through trauma that you will never understand.

The idea that you can't train an old dog new tricks is simply a myth created by people who were not up to the challenge. Dogs are much, much smarter than you think! They have an amazing ability to heal from trauma, both physical and emotional, as long as they have the right support system.

Hope is never lost, and every dog deserves a beautiful life and the opportunity to shine.

I have always had a love for the underdogs, the ones that have been abandoned, mistreated, and forgotten, the ones that have so much potential but are so often misunderstood! This love became a burning passion when I adopted my first rescue dog. It was game over as soon as I saw those big puppy dog eyes.

For the last 30 years, I have dedicated my time to learning different training techniques from various professionals in order to help my dogs and others to adjust to their new environments and become the loving companions they desperately want to be.

My goal is to guide you through how to overcome these challenges and provide you with tried-and-true techniques which will help you to untrain negative behaviors and replace them with much more family-friendly positive ones.

It is important to remember that this type of training doesn't happen overnight. It takes time, patience, and consistency. Do not expect Sam to be doing circus tricks by the end of this book! My goal is to assist you in providing the best possible life for your companion through training processes that will ensure you have the most enjoyable time together.

Before you start training, you need to understand your dog. Let's get started.

Chapter 1:

Walk a Day in My Paws

Dogs come in all different shapes, sizes, and personalities! Each one is completely unique and gifted with a variety of quirks you learn to either love or hate. It's important to remember that you are never going to be able to train out their personalities, and why would you ever want to?

Just like us, dogs find pleasure in different rewards and activities. You may have a dog that will jump through hoops for edible treats or a picky eater that only enjoys a specific food. I personally have a dog that goes mad for a ball and a chew toy and another who couldn't be bothered with either. However, as soon as he gets his jaws on a squeaky toy, he is in absolute heaven.

In this chapter, we are going to focus on how important it is to have a thorough understanding of your dog. Without it, your training experience is going to be incredibly difficult, and implementing big changes will be near impossible. Let go of what you think you know and allow them to direct you.

Understanding Your Dog

Understanding a dog is no easy task. It's going to take quite a bit of time and a lot of effort on your part. Wouldn't it just be so much easier if they could just talk about their feelings? At first, you may feel like you simply aren't getting through to them, but the more you train and bond, the stronger your relationship will grow. Through this, they will show you more and more of themselves. You just need to learn to listen and try to understand what they have gone through.

Rescued Dogs

Adopting a rescued dog is not as easy as it seems. Yes, you know that you need to get their medical history, make sure their vaccinations are up-to-date, and get them a collar with a cute little tag that has their name on it. However, there is so much more to it, and some of the below factors can often be overlooked amid the excitement of bringing your new friend home.

Background

Background history is absolutely vital. The rescue shelter will typically be able to provide you with an up-to-date medical history, but be sure to ask a few more questions to ensure you have a complete picture.

Has the dog suffered any injuries, and if so, from what? If these injuries have been caused by people or other dogs, you can already expect to deal with behavioral problems.

Next up, how long has the dog been in the shelter and why? Adult dogs are not readily adopted as they are not considered as cute, but there could be other reasons that factor into it, and the dog could have been returned before. The length of stay in a shelter also affects the dog's ability to quickly acclimate to a new home environment.

Lastly, and most importantly, what is the dog's temperament? Does it get along with other pets and people, and have there been any aggressive occurrences? For most people, this is make-or-break information, and dogs that have shown aggressive tendencies or fear toward people are not readily adopted.

Get Ready for Trouble

Prepare for the worst and be pleasantly surprised! Sometimes the background history you get is incorrect or incomplete.

Keep in mind everything that could go wrong and get yourself ready. Any animal that enters a new home and environment for the first time is going to be a bit scared. It's only natural! Be sure not to overwhelm them, as this can quickly bring about negative behaviors you aren't equipped to deal with just yet.

Introductions should be kept to an absolute minimum for the first few days. This includes introductions to other animals and strangers. I do not recommend that any new dog is left alone with young children or other pets until you are completely satisfied that they have adjusted and are comfortable.

It is common for a dog to go from an angel in the shelter to a little demon in your home. Their lives have been completely turned over, and it can take some time for them to fully recover.

Special Considerations

If you have chosen to adopt or have inherited a disabled or geriatric dog, fasten your seatbelts, as you could be in for a bumpy ride. First, I would like to thank you. These are such special souls and are so worthy of a happy, loving home. They are often so full of attitude and have amazing characters.

However, you will need to ensure that you are able to fully provide them with the correct care and attention they need. This is going to include special housing, food, medical checkups, and potentially, an overhaul of your house.

Many of the training techniques listed in this book can be adjusted to suit your special dog, but on the rare occasion, you may need to accept that your pet is not capable of change. This is when you need to adjust your expectations and figure out a way to live together comfortably.

Untrained Adults

You skipped a few puppy school lessons and didn't quite have the time to socialize your dog as much as you should have. No big deal, right? Well, if you purchased this book, you have probably realized that it is a bit more problematic than you thought. The good news is that training is going to be much, much easier as an established relationship is already in place, and your dog is living in comfortable surroundings.

Adult dogs are also likely to learn new commands and behaviors more quickly than puppies. This is mainly due to the fact that they aren't quite as distracted by every blade of grass around them.

Most of the work you will be doing with your dog will be behavioral correction. This will involve changing the negative behaviors they have learned to positive ones through positive reinforcement. You are usually the source of these behavioral issues, as they have learned that it is perfectly acceptable to behave like a monster in front of you. That may sting a little, but throughout this book, I will show you how important it is to work *with* your dog. That means that you might have to change too!

Breed Specific

In the dog world, we have used genetics to our advantage and bred individuals that possess specific characteristics together in order to produce different breeds that suit our wants and needs. Some dogs have been bred as workers, and some simply as companions with unique physical traits.

Each breed possesses its own set of traits, some negative and some positive. It is important to understand these traits in order to cater to their needs and find the right training methods.

Exercise, good food, boredom relief, and adequate attention are the four dog basics. Every single dog, regardless of breed, needs to have access to these four things in order to remain mentally and physically healthy. However, your breed may determine how much of each you will need to provide.

There are currently 360 recognized breeds worldwide, which is just way too many to discuss in one book. However, each of these breeds are placed into one of seven groups, determined by the American Kennel Club. Their grouping is determined by the original job the dog was bred to do. Let's take a look.

Sporters

If you are looking for highly energetic, fun-loving dogs, the sporters are for you! This group includes the pointers, retrievers, setters, spaniels, and the absolutely lovely Brittanies.

As highly alert dogs with a stable temperament, they were originally bred to be a hunter's best friend and were trained for hunting game birds. Retrievers were particularly sought-after, as they were always happy to brave the cold water to retrieve their prey.

What to Expect

In a home setting, sporters are generally considered fantastic family pets, as their goofy nature makes for great play time. They need to be provided with loads of exercise and activities to keep their minds sharp. Without this, they can begin to display destructive behavior out of boredom and frustration.

Hounds

Hounds can be split into two categories, scent hounds and sight hounds. Scent hounds are expert trackers that always have their nose to the ground. They are typically slower than sight hounds but more methodical. Bloodhounds, beagles, and bassets are included in this group.

Sight hounds are able to visually lock in on their target and use their long legs to reach amazing speeds in order to catch it. These breeds include greyhounds, whippets, Afghans, and wolfhounds. Due to their speed, these breeds are commonly used in sports such as dog racing.

What to Expect

Both groups are considered incredibly loyal and affectionate. However, their naturally strong prey drive can be difficult for some owners to navigate, especially if the dog has not been trained in recall. They are easily distracted by scents, sounds, and sights and will often become hyperfocused on their target. Once a hound locks onto something interesting, good luck getting them out of it.

Workers

As the name suggests, these breeds were made to work! Although the jobs they were given may vary from family and farm security to pulling sleds, they are all powerful, loyal, and protective dogs, which is why they seem to be happy working for free!

This group includes breeds such as Great Danes, mastiffs, boxers, huskies, and Bernese mountain dogs. These breeds are generally bursting with energy and are considered highly intelligent.

What to Expect

They were bred to work, and they need to be kept stimulated at all times. Mentally challenging activities such as food puzzles and regular training are great at curbing boredom and frustration. As large dogs, negative and destructive behaviors are much more noticeable and devastating. Regular, extensive exercise and a large play area are absolutely vital.

Herders

These farm dog breeds were bred to protect, gather, and herd livestock. Some breeds include shepherds, collies, sheepdogs, corgis and Catahoulas. These are all incredibly smart and naturally responsive dogs. Their alert nature and willingness to train has made them invaluable working dogs. They are commonly used in rescue and recovery teams, with police forces, and as service dogs.

What to Expect

Boredom sets in very quickly, and they require strict structure, regular exercise, and instruction to keep them in check. They thrive on mentally stimulating tasks, making training incredibly easy and fun. Agility training is a fantastic way to work with herders, as it keeps their minds sharp and provides an invaluable amount of exercise.

As loyal dogs, they are very protective of their owners and families. Don't be surprised to find your border collie herding your kids.

Terriers

Terriers can be split into three main categories. The short-legged terriers include breeds such as Scottish terriers and Boston terriers. These dogs were bred to hunt and kill small animals such as vermin that may wreak havoc in a farm setting.

Long-legged terriers such as miniature schnauzers and Jack Russells are in a similar line of work, but their long legs make them great diggers, and they were also used for game hunting.

Bull terriers such as the American pit bull and Staffordshire bull terriers were originally bred for bull baiting and dog fighting. Thankfully, we have left this terrible past behind and these breeds are now welcomed, loving companions.

What to Expect

Sadly, there is a stigma surrounding many terrier breeds, and a lot of people avoid adopting them because of it. The idea that these dogs are an inherent threat is completely inaccurate. No dog is born aggressive! Many of the behaviors dogs display are a direct result of their owners' teachings and actions.

All of these breeds are known for their confident and courageous natures, which makes them loyal and protective companions. They are energetic, fun-loving dogs that love nothing more than pleasing their owners. This makes them amazing family pets and even greater nannies!

Like all other breeds, they need structure, mental simulation, and regular exercise. Without it, they can be prone to negative behaviors such as barking and chewing in order to curb their boredom.

Toys

Toys include all the small, lap-sized breeds that were bred to be companions. Some of the most sought-after breeds include pugs,

Chihuahuas, Maltese poodles, Yorkshire terriers, shih tzus, and dachshunds.

They are affectionate, intelligent, and highly sociable with people and dogs alike. They adapt easily to different environments as long as they are introduced to that lifestyle when young. This makes them perfect traveling companions, and some breeds are even carried around in doggy handbags.

What to Expect

Small bodies, big personalities! These breeds can be stubborn and highly strung. They need regular exercise and mentally stimulating tasks to keep them happy. If you aren't an active person, you are in luck! Their tiny legs mean you only need to walk a couple of steps to keep up with exercise routines. They are highly affectionate and require a lot of attention. This makes them prone to destructive and attention-seeking behaviors if left alone without stimulation.

Teacup breeds can be prone to medical conditions such as physical injury, heart defects, and respiratory problems. This is due to their tiny size, and they should be fed a specialized diet to keep them healthy. It's important to keep an eye on them, especially around larger dogs and young children, and provide them with an appropriate play area as they can escape through small gaps.

Non-Sporters

Non-sporters include breeds that don't quite fit into the other categories. They are unique in the reasons they have been bred and can't really be compared to one another.

Due to the diversity of this group, we can't really discuss their common behaviors or what to expect when adopting. It's best to research each one to get a better understanding. For now, let's look at three different breeds from this group that couldn't be any more different from each other.

Dalmatians were originally bred as security guards for horses. They are extremely active and love the outdoors, making them perfect hiking partners. Their sensitive and playful nature makes them great household pets, though they may be a little too playful for small children. They are easy to train but require loads of exercise to curb destructive behaviors.

Poodles were originally bred as hunters but are now sought-after show dogs. Due to their highly intelligent minds, they are very easy to train and thoroughly enjoy mentally stimulating tasks. They crave attention and are prone to demand barking and destruction if left unattended for too long.

Bulldogs were originally bred for bull baiting. However, you would never think it with their sweet, easygoing nature. They are often mistaken for being lazy; however, they actually do enjoy walks when given the chance. They can quickly pack on weight if not appropriately exercised, which will make it much harder for them to curl up on your lap!

Start at Home

Now that you have a bit more of an understanding of your dog, you will need to figure out where you need to make changes in your life to accommodate them. These changes do not only apply to owners who have recently adopted or are planning to adopt an adult dog. These may also apply to those of you who are currently struggling with your lifelong pup.

Before you can even think of grabbing a leash and getting your dog out into the world, you need to focus on your homelife. Your home is your and your dog's safe place, and you need to structure it in a way that benefits both of you. That means boundaries!

Make the Changes

Dogproof your house! This is especially important for creating boundaries with new dogs. If there are certain areas of your home you would prefer your dog not to enter, find the best way to close off access. Many people do this through the use of baby gates, which are inexpensive and easy to set up. One of the benefits of using a baby gate is that your dog is still able to see what is happening on the other side. This can decrease anxiety in protective or needy dogs and reduce whining if used properly.

Use the remaining space to create a safe environment and remove any temptations from your dog's view. There are some things in this world that a dog just cannot resist, and at the top of that list is food.

You should pick one spot for your dog to eat, and I recommend that you use an area where they are isolated and able to eat in peace to avoid food guarding behavior.

Set aside a quiet space for them to relax and sleep. Whether you are using a crate or a bed, choose this space wisely. You don't want to have to move your dog around the house. This is tiring for you and disruptive for them.

Your dog needs potty breaks and exercise, so you will need to grant them access to your yard. Whether you are planning to allow your dog out without supervision or not, make sure that your fence is secure and high enough to avoid jailbreak situations. Don't underestimate what they are capable of! For some dogs, all it takes is one curious squirrel to kick them into Olympic level athletics.

It's Not Just About You Anymore

This is one of the hardest adjustments for new pet owners and parents. You can't just lock up the house and go on a three-day vacation anymore. Suddenly, you need to figure out how they are going to survive without you. Realizing that there is a little life that completely relies on you can be nerve-racking, and you are going to need to make some changes to your lifestyle to accommodate them.

Creating a routine will help both of you adjust to the new arrangement. Set a time for breakfast and dinner, a time for walks, and a time for play! You will be amazed at how quickly a dog can adjust to a new routine. If you set your play time for 3:00 p.m. every day, don't be shocked when you look over and find your dog staring you down with a tennis ball in their mouth at exactly 2:59!

Building a Family

You are not the only one who needs to bond with your dog. Everyone in your household needs to play their part in welcoming their new furry family member. Introducing an adult dog to your children should be done calmly and slowly. Ensure that your children understand what they can and can't do and show them how they can express their love in a way the dog can understand. Pulling a dog's tail is definitely not the best greeting!

The Foundations

When you ask somebody what the foundations of training are, you will likely receive a hundred different responses. Some might say it's down to commands and reward types. Some might say it's establishing dominance and creating boundaries. To me, there are four core fundamentals every dog owner should know. If you can live by them, you can train by them.

Love

There is absolutely nothing more important than love! It is the glue that holds the world together, and in your dog's eyes, you are that world. The bond between you and your dog will be the basis of all training. They need to be able to trust that you know what is right for them, and with that, they will readily learn from you.

Patience

This is a hard one! It can be impossible not to become frustrated when you're on your third load of soiled laundry. Throwing away the pillow that was unfortunate enough to become your dog's latest victim can quickly become the last step to full-blown tears, and that's okay! It is only natural, but it's important that you don't take this frustration out on your dog. Find yourself a coping mechanism, take a deep breath, and relax yourself.

When working with your dog, you need to be patient and understanding. They can quickly pick up on when you're feeling tense. This can put a damper on the activity, so you need to ensure that you are in the right mindset. If you are not feeling it, your dog probably isn't either. Ditch the work and skip straight to cuddle time.

Consistency

Establishing a routine is a great way to build confidence in your dog and secure a good relationship between the two of you. Remember to take it slow and don't make promises you can't keep. There is nothing wrong with missing a game of catch on a rainy day, but ending routines, especially fun activities, can lead your dog straight back to their old bad habits.

Consistency is also vital for training. You can't train for an hour and expect it to stick. Many of the commands you are teaching them are foreign, and you can't verbally explain to them why they are important to you. Instead, dogs learn through practice and positive reinforcement. The longer you keep it up, the more ingrained the behavior will become.

Time

Take your time when training. There is no way you are going to see results in one day, so don't try to push it. Dogs can get as tired and frustrated as you and will stop responding to your commands and rewards if they have had enough. Attempting to train during this time is only going to discourage them from learning.

Schedule an hour every day before playtime to train. Stick to using one command until it is fully ingrained, and then move on to the next. Slow and steady is the only way to win the race.

Chapter 2:

Behind Those Puppy Dog Eyes

Did you know that staring lovingly into your dog's eyes causes your brain to release a chemical called oxytocin? Also known as the love hormone, it's vital for bonding and gives you a sense of euphoria! Dogs are very in tune with their bodies, and while they may not understand why it is happening, they know that they love it. That is one of the reasons why some dogs crave attention from their owners.

As amazing as this bond is, you may be struggling with some of the behavioral issues that come with attention seeking. In this chapter, we are going to take a peek into your dog's mind and work through some of the most common behavioral problems and their potential causes.

You may be quite surprised! Sometimes all it takes to cure an undesirable behavior, is to remove the stimulus that is causing it.

Common Behavioral Problems

It is important to remember that at no point are dogs displaying behavior to purposefully irritate or harm you. Most of the issues we are going to talk about are behaviors that dogs have learned or are displaying due to another underlying cause.

The most common and probably the most frustrating behavioral problems include jumping, house training, barking, whining, pulling on their leash, and poor socialization, all of which will be covered in depth in this book at a later stage. However, there are a few others you may be dealing with.

Chewing

This is one of the worst! Coming home to pillow stuffing strewn around the house or your favorite pair of shoes torn to bits can be aggravating. It's a very difficult situation, and it's hard to not get angry. This sort of destructive behavior is usually from anxiety and boredom due to a lack of toys or mentally stimulating tasks. Ensure that your dog always has fun activities to do before you leave your home.

Some dogs are just natural chewers. Provide them with a ton of chew toys, lick mats, and interactive feeders to keep them busy. I always recommend that owners of chewers remove any temptations from their dog's area. If you know that they enjoy chewing shoes, don't ditch your boots right next to their bed.

Food and Toy Guarding

When you head to the kitchen, full of excitement, getting ready to savor that delicious piece of cake that you saved, only to find that somebody has already eaten it. The fury kicks in, and if you could, you would bite! The next time you get a piece of cake, you make sure to hide it or gobble it down immediately. Sharing is definitely not always caring.

Dogs that live in multi-pet households often feel the same way and this can lead to food, bed, and toy guarding. Food guarding can be solved by providing your dogs a safe space to eat without looming threats. If you are only feeding your dogs once a day, you may find they are even more protective of their food as they know it will be a while until their next meal. Spreading the meals throughout the day is a great way to solve this.

In order to prevent bed and toy guarding, you will need to give your dog a safe space in which to retreat when they are feeling overwhelmed or if they just want some alone time. Try to spread out your dog's beds or crates if you find that they are getting irritated with each other.

Begging

This behavior is regularly overlooked by owners. That is, until you have a dinner party and realize that your guests are getting continuously harassed by big puppy dog eyes. The number one reason for begging is you rewarding the behavior! Let's not pretend that you haven't slipped your dog some leftovers or a piece of juicy steak off your plate, so how can you be upset when they ask for more? The best way to solve this is to stop rewarding it.

If the behavior continues, add in a new step to your routine. At dinner time, get your dog used to being isolated from you, either in their crate or bed with a fun toy to distract them. Provide them with something rewarding other than your food.

Rough Play

Doggy play time is supposed to be fun, but it's less so when you come away with scratches and bruises. Rough play is pretty normal in the dog world, it just doesn't translate very well to humans. The best way to solve this problem is to approach it calmly. Teaching your dogs basic commands such as sit and stay can help you to refocus your dog and calm them before you continue playing.

Common Causes

There are tons of reasons your dog may be displaying negative behavior, and sometimes it is not easy to pinpoint. Trauma, medical complications, and abandonment are the most common causes, but other factors such as psychological disorders should not be quickly dismissed. You know your dog best, and it's important to trust your gut when it comes to identifying problems. If you feel as though there is something wrong that you are unable to fix, seek professional help from your veterinarian. They will be able to give your dog a full check-up and identify any physical or psychological concerns.

Nobody Taught Me Better

Dogs that have not been raised in a home environment are unlikely to understand your strange human rules. We live very differently from animals, and it can be a huge adjustment for them. When they see food, they eat it, not put it in the fridge and save it for later. When dealing with dogs like this, you need to go back to the basics and treat them the same way you would a puppy.

However, there are some dogs that have never really learned to be dogs! These are usually puppies that were removed from their mother and littermates too early. Their socialization skills are severely stunted, and they have never been taught boundaries. This is why it is never recommended to adopt a puppy under the age of eight weeks. During these fundamental weeks, your pup is busy testing the waters, biting their mom and littermates and getting put into their place. They learn to groom themselves and mom teaches them some basic safety rules. Most importantly, they receive their mother's love.

But the Others Dogs Do...

Most animals and humans learn through observation and imitation. As puppies, they learn important behaviors from watching their mother. As they grow, they become aware of the animals and humans around them and learn which behaviors and activities are treated as negative or positive.

If your dog sees another dog getting away with stealing food with no consequences, why can't they? This does not just apply to dogs that live in the same household. Some dogs may have never barked at people walking down the street or neighborhood squirrels, but when they see your neighbors' dog doing it, it seems quite fun, so why not join in?

Lack of Exercise and Mental Stimulation

Boredom is top on the list when it comes to behavioral problems. Dogs with no stimulation such as toys or interesting changes to their environment will be sure to find their own entertainment. The problem is, this kind of fun could be tearing up the couch and scratching down the doors. The same goes with exercise! High energy dogs are especially susceptible to behavioral issues when not exercised properly. There is no way for them to channel the energy that is bursting out of them, and they become increasingly frustrated. The way they display this frustration can be destructive and even dangerous. If they find that escaping the yard and enjoying an afternoon run is more rewarding than staying at home, it seems worth the punishment.

Thankfully, if this is the reason your dog is acting up, it is easily fixable with environmental and food enrichment and some good daily exercise.

Could It Be Medical?

There are many medical conditions that can contribute to undesirable behaviors. Some breeds may be prone to psychological genetic disorders such as obsessive disorders, while others may be prone to physical disorders such as hip dysplasia or hormonal imbalances.

No matter the medical cause, the concern remains that dogs are simply unable to communicate the issue with you! This is when you need to learn to listen through body language and carefully observe what they do when they don't know you are watching.

Pain

Dogs display pain in a few different ways. There are clear physical signs such as limping, visible injuries, and bleeding. However, internal pain is much trickier to communicate.

Whining is the closest way your dog is able to communicate with you. Think of it in the same way that you want everyone to know that you are miserable when you are down and out with the flu! This behavior can be very annoying, but if you continue displaying a negative reaction to it, your dog will stop trying to tell you what is going on.

Licking the same spot such as the stomach can indicate discomfort and pain. Dog's lick themselves to self-soothe, and if it brings them relief, this licking can quickly become obsessive. Licking and chewing paws can also indicate medical concerns like allergies, mites, and fleas.

Chewing on themselves or objects in the house is often a sign of a deep frustration, which can be brought on by pain. Puppies will typically chew everything they can get their paws on! This is because it brings relief during the teething stage.

Aggression is the most worrying sign of pain. This will usually occur when you touch a painful spot on their body, such as a sprained paw or a sore stomach. It can also be displayed if you are trying to get your dog to participate in an activity that they know will cause them pain.

Incontinence

A sudden onset of inappropriate urination and defecation in the house is regularly a sign of incontinence. This is typically common in aging dogs that are no longer able to hold it in for long periods of time. Your dog may also be suffering from a urinary tract infection. This will typically be accompanied by other behavioral symptoms such as whining and licking due to the pain.

Impaired Vision or Hearing

Being unable to see or hear properly is quite a terrifying thought. Dogs that are suffering from this typically become very alert of their surroundings, which enables them to navigate as normal. However, this can cause a lot of fear and anxiety, and if they get a fright, their body can switch them into fight-or-flight mode, and nipping can occur. Dogs with impaired vision are also prone to barking as they are unable to process the shadows they are seeing.

Rescue Trauma and Fear

Trauma can make us all do crazy things. Even if we don't realize what we are doing or why we are doing it, the fear can linger in your mind. Dogs feel the same way, but without having the ability to fully understand why they have been harmed, it can be difficult to bring them out of the pit and get them to trust again.

Dogs that have gone through trauma will often react in one of two ways when placed in the same or similar fearful situation: fight or flight.

Human-Inflicted Trauma

This can be the most difficult trauma to deal with! Dogs that have undergone trauma inflicted by humans can become wary or even aggressive toward owners, strangers, children, and even specific genders. More commonly, you may experience that your dog is fearful and cowers if you raise your voice or approach too quickly. Lying flat on the ground or belly up is typically a sign of submission, which is meant to tell you that they understand that you are in charge, and they don't want any trouble. This may seem harmless, but an overly submissive dog is not a confident dog.

Whichever behavior you are experiencing, it is important to take it slow and build up trust with your dog before introducing them to outside influences and strangers.

Dog-On-Dog Conflict

Trauma from a fight or attack from another dog can cause serious socialization problems. This is not always from a rescue situation. Inappropriate socialization methods can lead to arguments between dogs and cause them to become wary of others.

This can be a little trickier to fix. While you understand your dog and how they will react, you don't always know what the other dog may do.

Housing Trauma

This may seem a bit silly, but dogs can often display negative behaviors if they have been continuously displaced. This could either be due to a rescue situation or if you have had to move repeatedly over a short period of time. Your dog has not been able to fully settle into a place that they can call their home and territory, and as soon as they do, they are removed from it. This can cause increased anxiety as they never really know what to expect next.

Trauma can be healed through positive reinforcement, bonding, and love. However, it is not uncommon for owners to seek medical help for severely anxious dogs. This is a last resort, and you will need to work very closely with your veterinarian to ensure that your dog is receiving the correct treatment and making progress.

The Effects of Food

We read about it in magazines, watch it on TV, and are reminded of it on billboards. It's instilled in us when we are children. Healthy food is healthy living! Our bodies are organic machines, and without the proper food, we can run into all sorts of medical and psychological problems. We set out our eating routines, a protein-filled, grain-free egg and gluten-free toast for breakfast. Fruits packed with healthy sugars and energy for snacks sustain us throughout the day. A balanced meal of proteins, carbs, and vegetables that are full of vital nutrients fills us up for dinner.

Why do we not think about this when it comes to our dogs? Before you think about splitting your food with your dog, it's important to remember that their bodies require different levels of protein and nutrients to function correctly. They are simply not able to digest most of the foods we eat.

It can be a bit difficult standing in a pet store, staring at the shelves full of different brands of food. With so many options and so many price tags, how on earth are you supposed to choose? It's time to bring out the nutritionist in you and check the labels.

First things first, avoid dog foods that are high in carbohydrates, sugars, and filler ingredients. These are typically added to make the kibble seem more substantial at a much, much cheaper price. Eating this type of food is the equivalent to us living off of takeouts. Weight gain is always a concern, but you may find that your dog suffers from stomach upsets, urinary tract infections, and lethargy. Foods that are high in sugar can lead to hyperactive and destructive behavior, but once the sugar high begins to wear off, the crash begins and the moodiness comes out.

Protein is the most important ingredient in dog food. This is where your dog's energy comes from. Low protein foods will lead to lethargic or lazy behavior, which can often mimic depression. The right amount of fiber also needs to be taken into account, as this will keep your dog's tummy working the way it should. Without it, they may experience tummy upsets and constipation. Fatty acids and antioxidants are also common ingredients in high quality dog foods, especially puppy foods. These are used to promote healthy brain function and have been proven to assist in training and memory.

There are quite a few brands that create specialized foods for specialized breeds. These are readily available for owners of toy breeds.

If you are still struggling to decide, chat with your veterinarian. They will be able to direct you to the best food for your breed.

The type of food you give them is not the only factor that needs to be taken into account. Feeding schedules are also very important. We all feel that energy crash when we haven't eaten for a while, so imagine only eating one meal a day. A dog should be fed two to three times a day, the same way we feed ourselves. High energy dogs can even be fed four times a day. This reduces pigging out behavior and aides in proper digestion. It also keeps the metabolism and energy levels stable throughout the day.

Food should be correctly measured out for your dog's weight and energy levels, and this amount should be split evenly across all feeds. You will be pleasantly surprised at how a healthy, balanced diet can reduce behavioral problems in dogs. Only once their minds and bodies are healthy can you begin to work on correcting remaining behaviors.

Chapter 3:

Pawsitive Parenting

Negative reinforcement is a human nature default. When somebody does something wrong, you are confident enough to tell them that it's wrong, but how many times do you praise somebody for doing something right?

How many of you despise your boss because your hard work goes unnoticed, but if something goes wrong, you're immediately in the firing line? This is the same feeling many dogs experience. The only difference is that they can't leave the situation, go home, and vent about it to their partner.

In fact, it is often even worse for dogs, as they don't understand why the behavior they have exhibited is bad in the first place, especially if it is something they are doing to show you love. Negative reinforcement will typically lead to a strained relationship between an owner and a dog, which can negatively impact training. Positive reinforcement is all about killing negative behaviors with kindness. Promote the good, and the bad will soon cease.

What is Positive Parenting?

In order to truly understand what positive parenting is, you need to understand what it is not. In this chapter, we are going to run through a variety of parenting styles, conditioning, and training methods, and we'll discuss how to correctly manage your dog's behavior. It can get a little overwhelming at times, but don't worry! We will work through the methods again in the following chapters.

Parenting Styles

There are essentially three different parenting styles: authoritarian, permissive, and authoritative. Authoritarian owners use negative reinforcement, punishment, and dominance to stop their dogs from acting out undesirable behaviors. Permissive owners allow their dogs to do what they like without any consequence, essentially rewarding the undesirable behaviors.

Authoritative owners are in the middle, and this is considered the most effective, as it builds a strong bond between dog and owner while still maintaining structure and boundaries. Owners that use an authoritative parenting style will often follow the same principles of relationship-based training.

Relationship-Based Training

This training style incorporates a lot of different training methods which can be used to create a mutually beneficial life together. This requires having a clear understanding of how the dog feels when they are behaving negatively and trying to find and cure the source of the problem.

Training is done slowly, and the commands are usually taught in a quiet space so they are easy to retain. Once the command has been learned, the owner will begin to use the command in a more demanding setting. The difficulty of the training gradually increases as the dog becomes more comfortable.

Dominance-Based Training

This training is based on the concept of pack mentality within wild dogs and wolves, which relies on dominant and submissive behavior. In these packs, there is an alpha who essentially rules over the submissive individuals in the pack and directs them on what they can or can't do.

Dominance-based training mimics the same behaviors and reinforces the idea that you are above the dog, you eat first and walk through doors first. This also includes avoiding any behaviors that might make your dog see you as an equal, such as allowing them to sit with you on the couch or crouching down to their eye level. Some owners are known to hold their dogs down on their back to force submissive behaviors.

The biggest problem with this type of training is that you are not actually a dog. Why on earth are you acting like one? Your dog isn't fooled, and trying to mimic this behavior can cause aggressive responses resulting in bites. You are also reinforcing the idea of a pack mind, and if you are first, they will want to be second in command. If dominating your young child gives them an opportunity to achieve this goal, there is a good possibility they will try it.

This method is now considered outdated, and many behaviorists believe it creates a relationship of fear, which can be detrimental to training.

Operant Conditioning

There are four quadrants of operant conditioning. Positive parenting is all about using the least stressful, force-free methods which promote positive behavior. This includes positive reinforcement and, on occasion, negative punishment.

Positive Reinforcement

Positive reinforcement involves rewarding a desirable behavior with a treat or toy. In this way, the dog is more likely to repeat the same behavior. It is most commonly used in basic command training but is often overlooked when it comes to behavioral correction.

Negative Punishment

Negative punishment involves removing something desirable when a negative behavior is displayed. This training method can be useful if used correctly. A good example of this is closing your hand around a treat if your dog tries to jump up and snatch it instead of obeying the command you have given. An example of using this training method incorrectly would be removing your dog's access to food and water when they have a potty accident indoors.

Negative Reinforcement

Negative reinforcement involves removing something scary or aversive when a good behavior is displayed. This method involves the use of threats over actual punishment. Fitting a dog with a choke collar is a good example of this. If they display positive behavior by not pulling on the leash, you won't pull back and tighten the choke collar.

Positive Punishment

Positive punishment is the use of physical or vocal punishment methods to stop an undesirable behavior. This can be through yelling, jerking back on a leash, and hitting. Electronic training is unfortunately still widely used in today's society. It usually involves the use of a shock collar or similar device. When the dog displays a negative behavior, you can trigger the collar to shock them, punishing them for it. I highly suggest that anyone that purchases a shock collar tries it on themselves before inflicting it on their dog.

The only way for positive punishment to effectively work is by actively causing your dog enough harm or trauma to scare them out of a behavior. Otherwise, this method simply interrupts the behavior temporarily but never gets rid of it.

In some cases, positive punishment is a reward in itself. Dogs that are severely lacking attention may bark continuously. When you turn around and yell at them to stop, they may feel rewarded by getting your attention, even if it's negative attention.

For years, we have tried to train and command our dogs through negative reinforcement, punishment, and fear, but it has never worked as well as love and reward.

Dos and Don'ts of Positive Reinforcement

Do: Reward good behavior! This is how your dog knows they are doing something right. Rewarding your dog for obeying commands is not enough. You need to reward them for exhibiting positive behaviors all by themselves.

Do: Be consistent! Keep up with your training and routines and don't give in to temptation. You can't train your dog to stop jumping on the bed if you reward them for doing it when you want a cuddle.

Do: Be patient with your dog! They are trying their best, and this whole training thing is pretty confusing. Take your time and prepare yourself for them to make some mistakes.

Don't: Use force to train! This is not going to get you anywhere. If anything, you will be training your dog to fear the commands and behaviors you are asking of them.

Don't: Display negative energy! Dogs may not be able to talk, but they are very good at communicating through body language. When you are upset and tense, they are well aware of it.

Don't: Punish! I will say it again, using punishment to train a dog simply does not work.

Don't: Use harmful collars! Other than physically harming your dog, these collars can also cause great emotional trauma and make it very difficult for your dog to learn that walking is enjoyable.

Don't: Give in to frustration! You have got this. You are both trying your absolute best, and he is not doing these things to upset you on purpose. It's okay to feel upset; it's not okay to take it out on your dog.

Behavioral Correction Methods

When it comes to behavioral correction, there are a few different methods you can use. There is no one-size-fits-all style, and you will often find yourself needing to jump between different methods to remedy different types of behavior.

Extinction

Extinction is a type of nonreinforcement, which means that no negative or positive reinforcement is used to fix the behavior. All you have to do is ignore them.

By ignoring the behavior, you are not rewarding or punishing the act. You are simply reiterating the fact that what they are doing is not working. Once your dog realizes that they get absolutely no reaction from you, they will stop doing it, essentially rendering the behavior extinct.

This really doesn't work for dogs that are displaying aggressive or destructive behaviors, but it can be quite effective for minor issues. It has been used to remedy attention-seeking behaviors such as demand barking, jumping, pawing, and nudging.

The problem with using extinction as a correction method is that it is very difficult to keep up. The moment you acknowledge your dog when they paw you, you are reinforcing the behavior again.

Train an Incompatible Behavior

This method is very useful, and I recommend it over extinction, especially for attention-seeking behaviors such as begging. It involves training a positive behavior using something they enjoy, making it impossible for them to perform negative behaviors.

A very simple example of this would be training your dog to go to their bed and play with their toys. Each night before dinner, ask your dog to enact this behavior, and it will be impossible for them to beg at the same time.

Shaping

This is a great method to use for anxious and fearful dogs. It involves positively reinforcing everything but the undesired behavior. If your dog lies calmly in bed, reward them. If they sit and wait patiently without command, reward them. If they are fearful of a stimulus, reward them when they don't react!

This technique works by building up your dog's confidence, which allows them to comfortably complete normal activities and behavior while reducing the fear of a looming threat. If you plan to use this method, be sure to use vocal and toy rewards as well. If you only use treats, you are going to end up with a chunky dog!

Desensitization

Desensitization is usually used in conjunction with a clicker. This is most commonly used in dogs that are struggling with fear and fear-based aggression. The goal of this training is to desensitize your dog to the stimuli that scares or triggers them to react negatively.

This could include emotionally averse reactions to loud noises, people, animals, and even objects such as cars. Once your dog is comfortable using a clicker, you can begin to slowly introduce the negative stimulus. Each time your dog looks at you instead of the stimulus, you click and reward. This helps the dog remain calm and focused on you, and they will slowly begin to realize that the stimulus is not actually going to hurt them. This needs to be done gradually to avoid placing your dog into a state of high stress.

Change the Motivation

This is the easiest method of all, and it works almost every time. It involves changing the motivation rather than changing the behavior. For example, if your dog is restless and prone to barking and destruction at night, it is more than likely because they are still full of energy. This motivates them to display this behavior. Adequate exercise and stimulation throughout the day will tire your dog out. This sleepy feeling will motivate them to hop in bed and get some zzz's. Easy-peasy!

Model-Rival Training

Model-rival training makes use of observational learning. The idea is that if your dog observes you rewarding the model, a human or another dog, for a good behavior, they will mimic this behavior for the same reward. The model then becomes the rival, and your dog will try to compete against them to receive the reward first. This encourages your dog to complete the task quickly.

Management

Managing your dog's bad behavior can save you a lot of time and trouble. Removing the temptation that is causing the behavior will also remove the self-reward your dog receives from it. An easy example would be not leaving that delicious pepperoni pizza on the counter. If you are struggling with them wandering out the yard, fix your fence!

It seems so obvious, but we often forget that our dogs don't think the same way we do, and we need to be conscious of the temptations we are unknowingly putting in front of them.

Training Tools

Having the right training tools on hand is vital to the success of training. Dogs that feel uncomfortable or unmotivated are less likely to learn the behaviors you are trying to teach them.

Positive Parenting Tools

Treats

Having a variety of rewards is key, especially for dogs that can get easily bored. Not all dogs enjoy treats as a reward, and you may need to avoid them if you have a dog that is struggling with weight gain. This is where toys come in handy! Play time is just as rewarding as any tasty treat.

Walking Equipment

Having the right harness, leash, and collar for your dog can make a world of difference during your walks. Find something that suits your dog's temperament and most importantly, their size! Ill-fitting equipment is going to make for a miserable walk as your dog will be constantly trying to readjust the harness.

Clicker

A clicker is not absolutely necessary, but it really does make training much easier. They are quite cheap to purchase, so I suggest you grab one and test it out.

Treat Bag

Always have your treats handy! Holding multiple treats in your hand can be a bit confusing for your dog and will promote jumping up and grabbing. At the same time, stopping your training in order to go and get more treats from the kitchen can disrupt the learning process. A treat bag is a great way to store your training treats and keep them accessible by clipping the bag onto your belt.

Attitude

A good attitude is going to take you a long way. Your dog will pick up on your energy and match it, so if you are feeling excited and eager to learn, so will they.

The Dangers of Negative Reinforcement Tools

The biggest danger of using aversive tools is that they work—for a limited time. This reinforces us with the idea that they are good behavioral correction tools, and we continue to use them. The problem is, the dog will only suppress the behavior when the aversive tool is present. These tools do not help in long-term behavioral change.

A dog may walk calmly while wearing a choke collar because it is well aware that the threat of punishment is there. However, when walked with a normal collar, the threat is gone, and it's game on!

Shock, prong, and choke collars have the ability to inflict not only physical damage to our pets, but psychological damage as well. The constant fear of being punished for doing something wrong they don't know is wrong can be extremely traumatic.

Shock collars used for barking are especially damaging, as it is punishing the dog for exhibiting completely normal behavior. The dog may also associate the shock with the object, animal, or person they are barking at, causing a fear response when they are in their presence.

The use of aversion tools is the death of motivation. When there is no excitement or reward, and the only reason your dog is training is to avoid punishment, they will give you just enough to leave them be. Nothing more.

Heightened fear responses and anxiety will often lead to an increase in aggressive behavior. Remember, all dogs respond to fear by either fleeing or fighting. If the dog feels as though they are truly stuck in a frightening situation, it can turn aggressive.

Chapter 4:

The Crate Is Great!

I know what some of you are thinking. You will never use a crate! It's simply cruel. How could you put your dog into a prison like that? Well, I am here to assure you that that is simply not true, as long as you do it correctly.

Dogs, just like humans and other animals, need a space where they feel safe. a space they can retreat to when they are feeling afraid, tired, or simply done with you. All the crate is doing is mimicking the denning behavior of their wild counterparts, the wolves. The only difference is that this den comes with a fleece blanket and a bunch of fun toys.

By learning to use the crate to your and your dog's advantage, you can create a comfortable and safe home. It can also make the training experience a lot easier as it's a fantastic way to teach your dog, especially puppies, independence and boundaries.

Still not convinced? Let's dig a little deeper.

Why Crate Train?

First things first, the crate is a training and behavior management tool. It's your dog's comfort zone. It is not an easy way to control your dog by placing them into it for the day. They need exercise, stimulation, and space to thrive.

Your crate is a fantastic way to manage negative behaviors. If you are expecting visitors or have a nice dinner planned, you can put them into their crate with their favorite toy. This will stop them from jumping on your guests or begging for their delicious food. Rewarding them during this time will reinforce the positive behavior of remaining calm.

This is an ideal training method for teaching them boundaries and correcting negative behaviors such as potty mistakes, chewing, and attention seeking. By starting your new dog in a crate, you know that your house is safe. As your training progresses, and you start to get rid of the negative behaviors, you can gradually grant them more space by using a playpen around the crate. Open this space further until they are able to move around the house unsupervised.

Getting your dog used to feeling comfortable in a crate will also make traveling much easier. Whether it's by plane or car, you can always ensure that your dog feels safe and comfortable.

It's Not for Everyone

If you know that you are not going to be able to correctly crate train, don't do it! It requires time, energy, and your presence at home. If you struggle with time restraints during the day, consider doggy day care or a dogsitter. Another option is to use baby gates or similar devices to block off access to certain rooms of the house.

Some dogs don't take to crate training, at least not without extra help. High-strung and anxious dogs will struggle to be in the crate for long periods of time and may try to chew their way out if left unattended. This can lead to a greater fear response and cause your dog to view the crate as a prison cell. If your dog is suffering from severe anxiety, take training very slowly and avoid using training methods that could trigger them.

Setting It Up

Choosing Your Crate

There are a lot of different crates on the market. Some are cheap, and some are down right expensive! It all depends on what you need and what you are willing to spend. If you are still unsure about crate training or you only want to use it for a limited time, I suggest purchasing a mid-range crate. If you are planning to use a crate on a regular basis, do yourself a favor and spend a little more to get something you won't need to replace.

Size Matters

Purchase one that will suit your dog's size or is a little bigger to make sure they are completely comfortable. This is especially important if your dog is still growing. If you have a tail sticking out of one end and a snout sticking out the other, it is too small.

Consider Everything

What are you going to use it for? Is it just for home? Do you want to use it for transportation as well? Would you take it traveling? Purchase something that suits your needs. If you are undecided, there are plenty of versatile crates that can be dismantled and put up easily. Some of them are even adjustable to better suit your location.

The Best Materials

Crates can be purchased in four different materials: wood, plastic, metal, and fabric. Fabric crates are collapsible and easy to store. However, they are difficult to clean and do not work well for medium to large dogs. Plastic crates are generally used for travel purposes but can be used at home as well. They are durable and easy to clean, but can become quite hot and a little uncomfortable for your dog.

Wooden crates are great, but not commonly used in home environments. They are difficult to clean, especially if your dog has an accident, as the wood absorbs urine and odors. Dogs that are prone to chewing also tend to enjoy these crates as chew toys.

Metal crates are the most commonly used. They are durable and collapsible, so they can be easily moved. They are easy to clean and come with dividers or add on options which allow you to expand them as your dog grows.

A Safe Place

If the crate is not comfortable or in a good, peaceful location, your dog will not want to use it. It needs to be easily accessible so that if they want to, they can go and lie down on their own.

Location

Take your time to pick the right place in your house. You don't want it to be in a room that is very noisy, but you also don't want to isolate them completely. The living room is generally the best spot as this is where you will spend the most time together. Choose a shady spot. You don't want your pup to cook in the sun!

If you have two dogs that are besties, place their crates side by side so that they can keep each other company.

Making It Comfortable

Comfort is key! Use a soft padding on the base of the crate. This is especially important for heavy dogs. There is nothing worse than waking up with a sore back. Use your dog's favorite blanket and provide them with plenty of toys to play with. You will need to clean out the crate at least once a week and once a day if you are experiencing rain and muddy paws.

Training

Training your dog to use a crate is incredibly easy. As long as you keep your cool and reward the behavior, you can get them comfortable in just a few days. Before you start, make sure that your crate is fully set up and ready for use.

Step One: Introduction

Introduce your dog to the crate slowly; don't throw them in and close the door. Put treats into the crate or their favorite toy. Praise them each time they enter and give them a reward.

Some dogs may be apprehensive at first, and it can take some time for them to get in, especially if you are sitting behind them pushing their bums in. They need time to smell everything on the crate and ensure that it is not as dangerous as it seems. Lining it with blankets and pillows that smell like them will entice them in.

If they are really not interested, place something fun inside and walk away. Your dog may feel more comfortable to investigate when they aren't being intensely stared at.

Step Two: Close the Door

This is the trickier part. Only do this once your dog has settled in. Wait for them to get into the crate and provide them with something fun to do. You don't want your dog to focus on you at this point. If they are, they will want to push out the door to get to you. Once they are lying down and relaxed, close the door halfway. They may push back at first, and that's okay! Wait for them to relax and close it again.

Once your dog is calmer, close the door completely. I suggest sitting near the crate so your dog feels safe. However, keep your attention diverted. Read a book while you wait. If you focus on the crate, your dog will too.

Open the gate after a few minutes and repeat this step until your dog is comfortable.

Step Three: Walk Away

It's time to walk away! Your dog has felt safe with you near the crate, but as you walk away, they will quickly notice and try to follow you. At this point, I recommend that you put something really fun in with them. I love using lick mats as my dogs get completely engrossed in them.

Close the crate door and sit on the other side of the room. Again, don't concentrate on the crate or your dog. They may whimper for a second, but when they realize you are still there, they will relax and carry on playing. Repeat this step while moving further and further away from the crate until you are eventually out of the room.

Keep your cool. Your dog may start to whine, cry, and even panic when you leave the room. Resist the urge to don your superhero cape and sprint in to save them. Give it a minute or two and walk in calmly. Talk to them as you would just before play time, and then follow through with play time! You want them to think that what is happening is normal.

Common Training Mistakes

While mistakes are possible, they are also avoidable. Make sure you are training correctly and keep your dog's needs met.

Should I Be Worried Too?

Stop panicking and stop checking up on them! They can feel your apprehension, and they will match it. Keep up the encouragement and provide them with rewards. Make yourself some brownies and reward yourself if you need to. If you remain positive and confident, your dog will trust your decision.

I Don't Fit!

The crate is a relaxing, safe space where your dog can feel secure. It's not a prison cell. They need to be able to stand up, lie down, and move around in order to feel comfortable. A crate that is too small is going to lead to discomfort, body pains, and frustration.

I Need to Run!

Your dog needs to move. You need to let them out of the crate at regular intervals for them to stretch their legs, have a run, and go potty. Without this, you can expect weight gain, medical problems, and potty mistakes, not to mention a frustrated dog! With all that pent-up energy, you can expect them to burst out of the crate and never want to go back in.

This Is So Boring!

By not providing your dog with adequate stimulation, they are going to get bored! Don't expect them to sleep the day away. Bored dogs will begin to whine, bark, pace, and even try to escape. Give them their favorite toys and puzzles to play with to keep them happy.

What Did I Do Wrong?

It is important to remember that your crate is for management, not for punishment. Place them in the crate before your guests arrive, not after they jump! Using it as a punishment tool will cause them to have an adverse reaction to it, which can be difficult to fix.

Chapter 5:

Not on the Carpet!

Okay, let's be honest here. Is there anything more infuriating than standing in a puddle of an unknown substance? You close your eyes, take a deep breath, and try to pretend that it's anything else but pee, but you know the truth! The odor removers and sprays don't seem to be working, and you have never managed to catch your dog in the act to punish them.

We have all heard that rubbing your dog's nose in their urine is a sure way to get them to stop, but I mean, really? Imagine if somebody did that to you! This method is incredibly outdated, yet still widely used. Instead of fixing the problem, it instills your dog with fear, and all they understand is that urinating is bad.

This often leads to dogs feeling the need to hide from their owners when they need to potty. This can cause more accidents in the house and greatly affect their ability to potty during walks and play time.

The good news is that there are very easy ways to potty train your dog, even when they are fully grown. However, it requires you to take a couple more deep breaths, prepare for a couple of accidents, and for the sake of your dog, avoid punishment!

Why Is This Happening?

There are many reasons why this behavior could be happening. We will go through a few of the most common ones and then figure out the best way to curb the behavior. Some solutions may be simple and some less so. It is all going to depend on how ingrained the behavior has become.

I Couldn't Hold It Any Longer

Incontinence is incredibly common in aging dogs. Some breeds may reach this stage in their life earlier than others. It's always important to keep up with regular health checks, especially when they are reaching their golden years, to ensure they are comfortable and happy.

If your dog is younger and has suddenly begun to display this behavior, it could be due to an injury or infection. Monitor your dog and check for any signs of uncomfortable or painful behavior that usually accompanies an infection. When in doubt, check with your veterinarian.

Where Is All My Stuff?

Moving may be exciting for us, getting to start fresh in a brand-new place, but this is absolutely terrifying for dogs. They are moving to an unknown location with no idea why. They don't know the new setup, their usual poopy place outdoors is now gone, and there is still the lingering smell of the last dog that lived there. It is perfectly acceptable for your dog to make a few mistakes during this time, so bear with them and help them navigate the new environment.

I Didn't Know It Was Bad

This is most commonly seen in rescued dogs. They have never had to learn human etiquette, so they have never had to learn to potty outside. Dogs that have lived in shelters for a long time are typically not provided with large enough areas to make the association to potty outside, sleep inside. Their outdoor area is just next to their resting place. So when they move into a new home, they think they are doing pretty well making sure that they poop 5 feet away.

How Do I Get Out of This Place?

Dogs that have never lived indoors are typically very uncomfortable pottying inside. While outdoors, they have had the opportunity to go whenever they needed to, no waiting and no permission needed. Indoors, they need to learn to grasp the new concept of asking to be let out and learning how to hold it in until they have the opportunity. Your dog is guaranteed to make mistakes indoors until you are able to establish a new routine.

This Is MY Space!

Dogs will often mark their territory during walks and while visiting the park. This is to show everyone they have been there and that they own that tree! At home, your dog does not feel the need to replicate this behavior, as their presence is already firmly established. However, this behavior can be triggered by bringing home a new furry family member.

Your dog may feel threatened and feel the need to reinforce the fact that this space is theirs and theirs alone. It's important to help your dog feel comfortable and safe during this turbulent time by providing them a private space they can call their own. Introduce the new dog slowly and keep them away from your dog's safe space in the beginning. Once the stress subsides, the behavior will generally stop.

I Missed You So Much!

Some dogs urinate when they are excited to see you. This is called submissive urination, and it is a perfectly natural behavior which is mostly displayed by puppies. As nice as it is to know that somebody loves you enough to pee themselves, you also really don't want to be the one that has to clean it up. This behavior usually subsides as your dog grows up, but smaller toy breeds may continue it into adulthood.

Why Didn't You Listen?

Let's be honest. How many of you have been lying comfortably in bed, about to fall asleep, and your dog begins to whine? You wrestle with the pros and cons of ignoring it and by the time you finally get up, you realize your dog couldn't wait any longer. You need to take responsibility in situations like this. It's your job to create a structured routine that ensures your dog has enough time outdoors to do their business—especially before bedtime!

How to Tell When Your Dog Needs to Potty

Most dogs are relatively vocal when it comes to telling you they need to go outside. They will often whine, bark, or scratch at the door. Quiet dogs may pace around the room, circle certain areas, or sniff around the floor looking for the best spot to potty. The quietest ones are the ones that suddenly sneak out of the room after making sure you aren't watching.

Get to know your dog and their tell-tale signs so that you can judge when you need to take them outside. If they realize that whining gets you to open the door for them to potty, they will learn to continue using that cue to communicate with you.

The Solution

When it comes to training or correcting any kind of behavior, we need to give a little to get a lot. Typically, the giving part involves changing parts of our environment and routine to accommodate our dog and assist them in their learning. It's important to find a mutually beneficial way to do this so that you don't end up feeling uncomfortable.

Organize Your Home

Start inside and work your way out. You need to make a few small changes indoors to disrupt the habit. These changes are usually reversible once the behavior has been corrected.

Sterilize, Sterilize, Sterilize!

First up, clean up the mess. The smell is gross enough for you, but any lingering scents can trigger your dog to potty again in the same place. There are lots of commercial pet odor products you can use to clean these areas, but a homemade mixture of white vinegar and water works just as well! White vinegar contains acetic acid, which can be used to remove alkaline odors. Soak any linen items in this mixture as well before washing them with normal laundry liquid.

If your dog has messed on items you cannot remove or soak, such as a couch or a carpet, you can use baking soda. Sprinkle the baking soda over the area and leave it to absorb the urine for at least five hours. You can then vacuum the remaining powder and clean the area with a normal upholstery or carpet cleaner. If you find that the smell still lingers, you can repeat the baking soda trick and spray the area with vinegar.

Restrict Access to Certain Areas

Dogs are creatures of habit and will often use the same spot to relieve themselves. If your dog has taken to pottying in certain areas of the house, especially carpeted areas, it's time to revoke their access. If possible, keep these areas blocked off either by closing doors or using baby gates. Make sure that your dog still has adequate space in the house to play and access to the yard.

Restricting access to their usual toilet will disrupt this routine and open up the door to learning a new one.

Indoor Potties for Aging Dogs

If you find that your aging dog is struggling to hold it in at night, it's time to make them an indoor potty area. It's not ideal, but it is much better than scrubbing a carpet every morning! Choose your spot wisely. You don't want it right next to your bedroom, and you want to be able to sterilize it daily. If your dog has taken to using a certain area already, it's worth turning that into their nighttime potty.

At night, lay down newspaper, artificial turf, or puppy training pads. Use anything that is absorbent, and your dog will readily take to it. In the morning, clean and remove the items to encourage your dog to potty outdoors.

Routine

Routine is everything! You need to provide your dog with enough opportunities to display good potty behavior to develop a routine together. They can't pick and choose when they need to potty. Their bodies are doing that for them based on the food you are providing them. At the end of the day, they are going to be the ones dictating the routine, you just have the opportunity to slightly adjust it.

Feeding Schedules

Get your feeding schedules right. Dogs should be fed two to three times a day, the same way that we eat. Food goes in, food gets digested, food comes out! This all happens in the space of a couple of hours, so meals should be given at a reasonable time every day. If you only feed your dog at 9 p.m., they are going to need to potty by 1 a.m., and if you are not awake, you can't blame them for messing in the house. The same goes for breakfast. Feed them as soon as you wake up and allow them outdoors for a final potty break before you leave for work.

Don't Be Lazy, Open the Door!

Set up a regular schedule so that your dog has options. The most important times are going to be as soon as you wake up, after every meal, a midday break, and just before bedtime. For dogs that are still struggling to get into routine, give them an opportunity every one to two hours.

This does not have to be a full walk. It can just be taking them outdoors. If they don't need to potty after five minutes, bring them back inside.

Keep Track

Get yourself a notepad and make a doggy potty book to keep track of your dog's poops. Okay, you don't really need to go that far, but at least make mental notes of when your dog does its business. This will help you get a better idea of when you need to schedule your walks and potty breaks. Once you figure this out, you can slowly wean off the hourly potty sessions.

Nighttime Potty Breaks

Let your dog out to potty right before bed, and I mean right before! Once you shut the door, you should be turning the lights off and getting into bed. Letting them out an hour before bedtime is not enough, especially if they have decided to drink some water or nibble on food before they go to sleep. If you sleep for eight hours, your dog needs to hold it in for eight hours. Keep this time gap consistent with the amount of hours you're asleep, and this should be enough to avoid any nighttime mistakes.

You are going to have to avoid the luxury of sleeping in, at least until your dog is fully trained.

Reward the Behavior

Always reward the good behavior. Don't punish the bad. When your dog successfully potties outdoors, make a big scene! Tell them how fantastic they are, give them a treat, and reward them with some play time after each potty break. They will soon learn that you really like it when they poop, and they aren't too fussy about asking why.

By ignoring this behavior when it happens indoors, your dog will learn that they get no reward, and it's not worth their time if they have an opportunity to go out and get praised. Punishing the behavior when it's indoors and praising it when it is outdoors is very confusing. They are not sure if they are being punished for being inside, the exact spot inside they chose to potty, or if you changed your mind about being happy that they pottied at all. Sometimes, they don't even associate the punishment with it!

It is helpful to use a clicker or a cue word such as "go potty" when training. Clickers are great because your dog will identify the exact behavior they are being praised for. Keep it on you when you leave the house and use it the moment they are finished.

Use a Crate

If you have decided to crate train your dog, the steps above are going to be a lot easier. As discussed in the previous chapter, the crate allows you to restrict access, which means your dog doesn't have the option of sneaking off to potty. They will have to communicate with you.

Put your dog in their crate when you are not playing or working with them. Give them a break every hour and take them outdoors for an opportunity to potty and stretch their legs. As your dog starts to learn that this behavior is rewarding, you can start granting them more access to the house.

Do this by adding a playpen or baby gates around the crate. This now gives them the opportunity to potty outside the crate. However, they should have learned that this is not acceptable behavior. If they continue to display good toileting etiquette, you can expand their indoor space!

Chapter 6:

Eyes on Me!

Now it's time for the fun part, training your dog to obey commands. This is one of the most rewarding experiences, and most dogs are able to pick up what you want from them very quickly. This is not just training; it is bonding as well. The two of you will learn invaluable information about each other through the process and build a much stronger relationship.

While "sit" and "lie down" are usually viewed as cool little tricks you can teach your dog and use on the odd occasion you want to show them off, they are actually much more meaningful. These commands are going to form the basis of the rest of the training covered in this book.

Dogs, just like people, learn through repetition, and they are perfectly capable of forgetting something that has not benefited them in a long time, which is why it is so important to continue training these commands throughout your dog's life.

Choose Your Rewards

Picking the right reward will make all the difference in your training efforts. Treats are usually the go-to reward, but if you are trying to get active and train an overweight dog, these are going to be a big no-no. Some dogs will also respond better to toys or vocal rewards. Believe it or not, dogs can get bored when they have had too much of a good thing. Keep a variety of rewards on hand and alternate between them to keep the excitement alive!

Treats

Pick your treats carefully. You want them tasty but healthy! Avoid treats that are loaded with sugar and carbohydrates, and opt for protein-filled grain-free ones which promote mental and physical health. Larger treats such as biscuits and chew strips are great options for home. However, when it comes to training, your dog is going to gain a ton of weight if you are offering them a full biscuit for every good behavior they display.

Purchase specialized training treats, make them at home, or break up your larger treats into small pieces. Your dog is not looking for a gourmet meal to savor. Lots of small rewards work better than one big one, and pieces a little bigger than a grain of rice work perfectly.

Toys

Choosing toys can be a little trickier because different dogs like different things. I am sure you have purchased some toys that you thought were great, but when you offered them to your pup, they just gave you a blank stare, wondering how you could be so stupid to think they would like things like that. I suggest that you buy one toy of each variety and test them out with your dog to see what they enjoy. You will need to purchase toys for solitary play and communal play.

Chew toys are for solitary play. They are great for natural chewers, puppies, and dogs that are easily bored when alone. Squeaker toys are also fantastic for solitary play, but this depends on how much squeaking your ears can actually take.

Enrichment toys such as food puzzles and treat dispenser balls are vital for dogs that need constant mental stimulation. I am looking at you, border collies! Most of these have an option for adjusting difficulty levels to ensure your dog does not get bored with them too quickly.

Communal play toys such as balls or Frisbees for fetch provide your dog exercise, and the fun play time can help you bond. Tug toys are very popular options to use as rewards when playing. You still stay in close contact with your dog, and you can easily remove the reward when you want to perform the behavior again.

Vocal Rewards

Vocal praise is just as important as any treat. Pair your praise with rubs and pats to get an even better response from your dog. Try to use the same phrase and voice pitch to praise your dog. This will help them associate the words with the good behavior.

Clicker Training

Clicker training is incredibly useful when using positive reinforcement methods. When a dog displays a good behavior, you click and reward. The advantage of using a clicker is that it immediately signals that you approve of the behavior. This allows for quicker learning as there is no gap between behavior and reward in which the dog could get confused.

In order to use a clicker, you need to first teach the dog that the click means reward. All you need to do is click, treat, click, treat, and within minutes, your dog will understand exactly what it means. Once they have been conditioned, you can begin to use your clicker in conjunction with other training methods.

Command Foundations

Sit

"Sit" is definitely the most frequently used command in dog training. Dogs are basically preprogrammed to obey this command. That's how easy it is to teach. This is usually taught to puppies as a cute little trick, but it is actually much more important. Not only does it form the foundation of all other training methods, but it also immediately stops any unwanted behavior. Your dog can't jump, pull on the leash, or sprint out the door while they are sitting! Using this command immediately calms them and brings their full focus back to you.

How-to

1. Grab some treats and move into a quiet space with no distractions.

2. Stand in front of your dog and get their attention by showing them the treat.

3. Hold the treat up over their heads out of their reach and slowly move your hand toward the back of their head.

4. Say the word "sit."

5. As you move the treat further back, they will be forced to sit in order to keep it in view! Repeat "sit."

6. When their bum hits the floor, click and treat!

7. Repeat these steps until they choose to sit before you get a chance to say your cue.

Down or Lie Down

Now that your dog is sitting like a champ, you can move onto the "down" or "lie down" command. It is up to you to decide which cue to use. I prefer to use "lie down" to avoid confusion, as I use the cue "down" for when my dogs try to jump. This command also forms the foundations of the tricks used in agility or sport training.

It is a lovely command to use for anxious or overly excited dogs, as it's a quick way to get them to relax. It works especially well for car rides and vet visits. The effectiveness of this cue, of course, depends on your dog's personality.

My pup is so eager to please that he will often perform "sit," "paw," and "down" in a matter of seconds. This voids the idea of using this cue to produce a calming behavior. When practicing multiple commands, I now say, "Hit the deck!" I use the cue "calm" to get him to lie down and relax in everyday scenarios.

How-to

1. Grab your treats and move into a quiet location.

2. Show them the treat and ask them to sit.

3. Touch your treat to their nose and move it down to their paws.

4. Once they start to bend down for it, slide it along the floor in front of them and say the commands "lie down" or "down."

5. When they lie down to reach it, click and treat!

6. If they stand up to follow the treat, move them back into the sitting position and start again.

If your pup is still struggling to understand what they should be doing, place your hand on their lower back and gently apply pressure at the same time that you move the treat away from them.

Stay

Sit and down are pretty pointless if your dog doesn't understand that they need to stay in that position! When you want your dog to remain calm, get them into a lying down or sitting position and ask them to stay. When practicing "stay," you can also incorporate the command "come," which will better prepare them for recall training.

How-to

1. Get your dog into a sitting position and hold your palm out toward them in a stop motion.

2. Say the command "stay" and slowly back away from them, repeating the cue word.

3. If they get up to move toward you, tell them to stop with the command "uh-uh" or something similar. I don't really like to use the word "no," but you may if you choose. Once they are sitting, continue to move back slowly.

4. When you are ready, tell them "come" or "okay" and reward them!

5. Repeat the steps above while increasing the distance between you each time.

Come

Recall is not optional. It is vital! If you are unable to get your dog's attention back onto you, you are in for a world of trouble when you start walking. This is especially important if you have a reactive dog or if you want to get to the point that you can walk without the leash. It is often overlooked in training, which is ridiculous, because it's so easy to teach. It just takes some patience.

How-to

1. Find a quiet spot outdoors where there are no distractions.

2. Hold your leash but keep it loose. Grab a handful of treats and face your dog.

3. Hold them in a sitting position and tell them the command "stay."

4. Move back quickly and say, "Come!" They will run toward you, and you are going to need to give them a big reward. I'm talking, cheers, jumps, treats—everything you have in your reward arsenal. You need them to think that coming back to you when called is the best thing since sliced cheese.

5. Repeat this a few times. Making your runs a little further each time.

6. Change from rewarding them with treats to one of their favorite toys. When they come to you, play with them for a minute or so.

7. If you are practicing this in your backyard. You can start to repeat the steps without your leash.

8. When you feel confident that your dog is obeying, add in some distractions. Start by getting a friend in, they should be standing a few paces away and doing something intriguing. They cannot call your dog toward them, as this can cause a bit of confusion.

9. Once your dog starts to walk toward them, say, "Come!"

10. Practice this during your walks, especially if you find that your dog has become interested in something.

11. When they return to you, reward them! Remember to reward your dog only when the leash is loose.

Heel

Want to get your dog walking nicely? Teach them to heel! If you can get this down before your walk training, you have won half the battle.

This is a great way to create a bond between you and your dog, as they will learn to trust your decision-making and keep their focus on you.

How-to

1. Clip your leash onto your dog's harness, grab your treats, and find a quiet space outdoors.

2. Stand with your dog on your left-hand side. You want your leash in your right hand and your treats in your left so that your dog can see them.

3. Hold a treat close to your body but in front of your dog's face. Take a step forward and say the command "heel." When they walk with you, click and reward them.

4. Take some more steps, giving them a reward each time they obey the "heel" cue. If they wander off, call them back and get them to sit before you start again.

5. Once they get the hang of it, place your treats into your pocket so that they are out of view. Increase the number of steps you take before you use your command and reward.

6. Up the difficulty by practicing this in a new setting that has more distractions.

Drop It!

This command is fantastic to get your dog to stop trying to kill themselves! Use it to stop negative behaviors, such as chewing, by getting them to drop the shoe they were about to destroy. Or use it to stop them from stacking up expensive vet bills by getting them to drop the batteries they wanted to eat for lunch.

This training session is going to be about trading. You will need to give them something nice and ask them to drop it for something better.

How-to

1. Start by giving your dog a toy. It should be something they enjoy, but it also can't be their favorite one. Allow them to play with it for a bit.

2. Whip out the delicious treats and place one in front of their nose while saying, "Drop it."

3. If they drop the toy, click and reward them with the treat.

4. Take the toy away from them while they are enjoying their tasty snack.

5. Give them back their toy and repeat the process as many times as needed.

6. You can start upping the difficulty by replacing the toy with something they like better. If your dog loves playing fetch, practice getting them to drop their ball.

Leave it!

Once your dog has figured out that they need to drop something, you can start to use the cue "leave it" to prevent them from picking up the object in the first place. If you own a dog that has a strong prey drive, this command is vital, especially when they catch sight of another animal.

How-to

1. Move to a calm location and ask your dog to sit.

2. Close your hand around the treat and allow your dog to sniff your fist. They should start trying to take it from you.

3. Say the command "leave it," and when your dog stops trying to take it from you, click and treat!

4. Repeat this a few times until your dog gets the hang of it.

5. You can now up the difficulty by showing them the treat! Open up your hand and say, "Leave it." If they try to take the treat, close your hand until they sit back down.

6. When they leave the treat in your open hand, click and treat! Don't reward them with the treat you are holding. Grab another one with your free hand.

7. Make it a little more difficult by placing your practice treat by your feet. If they try to grab it, cover it with your foot.

8. When they leave the treat alone, click and treat!

9. If they are doing well, you can start to back up a little so that the treat is fully exposed. If they try to go for it, make sure you get there first!

It's important to always reward your dog with something other than your practice treat. If you allow them to take the treat that you asked them to leave, they will think it's fine to pick up any object you ask them to drop after they have obeyed you.

Rinse and Repeat

You are going to need to practice these commands over and over again for your dog to fully understand what you are asking them to do. This means that you can't just use these commands during practice sessions or to show off how smart they are to your friends. You need to incorporate them into everyday situations. Leave a plate of food on the table, and when you see your dog approaching, tell them, "Leave it!" If they obey, reward!

These little exercises will not only ingrain the commands, they will also be great opportunities for short bonding sessions, especially when your dog is getting rewards out of them.

Some dogs take a little longer to figure it out. Don't give up! They aren't stupid; they just don't speak human. If you have another dog that performs the behavior you want, you can practice with both of them at the same time. Dogs are brilliant at learning through observation.

Chapter 7:

Painful Greetings

There is nothing like being slammed against the wall by a raging 80-pound dog that can't contain their excitement to see you. While we wish that everyone in our lives would be this happy to see us, it can get to be a bit much, especially when you're wearing your new white pants.

While this behavior is frustrating, you need to remember that most of the time, your dog is just doing this because they love you. Let's be honest, how many times have you encouraged it when you were just as excited to see them?

We have all heard that the best way to stop a dog from jumping is to pull your knee up and hit them in the chest. Imagine getting punched in the ribs by somebody you love because you were trying to give them a hug. It doesn't seem as reasonable when you turn the tables.

As with all my training methods, we will focus on killing the negative behavior with kindness. There are loads of ways your dogs can tell you that they are happy to see you. You just need to teach them how.

Why Is This Happening?

Why is my dog committed to tearing me to shreds with those sharp claws? Let's take a look at some of the most common reasons and then try to figure out how to make it stop, preferably while you still have some good clothes left.

Hi! Hello! Hi!

The excitement of seeing their owner after they've been gone for years (okay, it was just five minutes) is often too much for your dog to take. Your dog loves you, and they want you to know it by giving you a big, slobbery lick on the face. This is typically very rewarding for us, at least until it starts to hurt, or when you're in a sour mood. This is generally a bigger issue in large dogs, especially heavyweight champions such as Great Danes, who can knock you off your feet. Let's not forget that their small counterparts jump just as much. The only difference is that they can only get up to your knees.

I Just Want You to Know That You Are Mine

Jealousy makes you nasty. If you are in a multidog household, you have most definitely dealt with jealousy jumps. You give one dog a quick loving glance, and sure enough, you have three more dogs on your lap looking for some of that sweet affection.

This kind of territorial behavior can transfer onto people as well. Yes, your dog can become jealous of your spouse! They want to make sure that everyone around knows that you are theirs and theirs alone. This often occurs if you have allowed your dog to take over or share every aspect of your life, like allowing them to sleep on your bed, eat from your plate, or display any behavior they want and get away with it. When somebody comes in and threatens that relationship, they are going to fight to save it.

Boundaries

Getting your dog to understand that you are allowed to love other people can be tricky. You are going to need to set some boundaries, but these need to remain consistent. You can't go back on the rules you have put into place when your spouse leaves for work.

Stop your dog from performing activities that could create a rift between you and the person you love. An example of this would be your dog jumping on the couch and sitting between you. The solution would be not to allow the dog on the couch or to make your dog sit on a designated seat. Allowing behavior like this or laughing it off as cute is going to reinforce your dog's jealousy.

When you play or train, you all need to work together. Allowing your dog to develop a relationship with your partner independently is vital. Leave the room and allow them to get to know each other.

Please Play With Me!

If you ignore them long enough, you're sure to receive a slap. Or a kick? A nudge, perhaps. Regardless, your dog may find assaulting you the easiest way to get your attention, and oftentimes it works. One of my lovely rescued pups immediately took to nudging me under the arm when he wanted a cuddle. However, just like all bad behaviors, it started out cute, and then I found myself covered in boiling hot coffee.

The best solution, here, is to ignore the behavior and stop rewarding it. Turn away from them so they can't jump. If the jumps are becoming a bit much, you can gently push them down by applying some pressure to their chest.

I Am So Excited, I Could Jump!

Dogs get pumped up when they know something exciting is about to happen. They need a way to express how they are feeling. They might jump or bark or zoom at light speed around the house. It just depends on their personality. It is really unfair to take away their feelings of excitement, and it's important that you allow them to express themselves. Of course, it becomes a problem if they're jumping on you, but if they aren't harming you, and it's not an excessive behavior, then let them enjoy life!

Don't Get Caught up in the Excitement

Enjoying your time with your dog is one thing. Riling them up to display negative behavior is another. Remain calm and treat them the way you want them to treat you. If they get too excited during play, slow it down a little. You both need to refocus and take a breath before starting up again.

Oh, You Like This Now?

Consistency, consistency, consistency! If you don't want your pup to jump on you, don't encourage them to. A lot of owners encourage jumping when it's beneficial and rewarding to them. Lapdog-sized pups are irresistible and, of course, you want to pick them up and get a heartwarming cuddle. You can't blame them for trying to get back into your arms the next day. No jumping means no jumping!

This means that your family and friends need to be aware of and on board with your training methods. It's not okay to jump on one person and not the other. Some dogs may make the connection, but most do not, especially when the excitement hits. Whip out that whiteboard, get your laser pointer and give your visitors a full military briefing on what to expect and what not to do.

Please, Just Stop

Most of the behavioral causes above are based on love. Do not punish your dog just because you've had a hard day! Direct them on the best way to show their feelings by rewarding the good behavior.

Manage It!

Keep your treats on hand or leave a tub of them near the door. When you arrive home, and they start to bounce off the walls in excitement, grab a treat! Give them a command to do something positive, such as "sit," "get your toy," or "go to bed," and reward them for obeying it.

I personally found that using the command "toy" has worked wonders for my dog. He used to jump and kiss everyone that walked through the door. Now he grabs his favorite squeaker toy and shows it off before heading back to bed to play. The excitement is still very much there! His tail wags so hard that his entire body moves with it. We are still able to greet him with excitement so that he knows we missed him too. The only difference is the energy is now directed into the toy.

If you have a crate, use it! Before your guests arrive, pop your dog in, and voilà! You have avoided disaster. If you have designated a specific area for your dog to stay in while you are away, make sure they don't have access to the front door. Block this off so that you can walk in peacefully. Greet them over the gate and reward them for sitting calmly.

Sit Means Sit

Now, it's time to get down and dirty with training. Your leash is going to be an important component here. It allows you to easily control your dog's behavior and redirect them when they display negative behaviors. Put on some dog proof pants and grab your treat bag.

Step One: Gain Control

Get your dog into a sitting position and stand on their leash. They need enough leeway that they can move but not enough so that they can jump up onto you. Greet them. If they jump, ignore them or gently push them down by applying pressure to the chest. This is not reinforcing the behavior. It's managing it.

Step Two: Reward Good Behavior

When they sit, treat! Greet them again. Reward them for easy wins at first. When they start to get the hang of it, you can wait a little longer between treats, but make sure that you are not taunting them. Keep the treats in a treat bag or in your pocket and take out one at a time. If you are holding a bunch in your hand, and you are not rewarding the behavior, you are asking for a jump.

Step Three: Up the Difficulty

It is time to ditch the leash and add in a little more excitement. Greet them as usual. If they sit, reward them! You can start to move around the room, turning to greet them at semiregular intervals. If they jump on you, you now have two options. You can either turn around and ignore them until they are sitting, or you can gently push them down as before. Wait for them to sit and reward them. Rinse and repeat.

Remember, this is not going to stop the behavior immediately. This takes time and practice.

Step Four: Bring in a Guest

If you are feeling confident in your training and the way your dog has behaved, you can add a guest to the equation. Gather up the leash and stand with your dog next to you.

Get your visitor to stand at a distance. When your dog is sitting or looks at you for direction, treat them. Ask the visitor to approach slowly. If your dog stands up, your guest needs to stop, and you need to redirect your dog into the sitting position. Once that bum is on the floor and they look at you, treat them!

Continue this until your guest is able to walk up and greet them with some gentle pats.

Bring It All Together

When you know your guests are arriving, start by managing your dog's behavior. Distract them with a toy or a treat, or by placing them in their crate or another room. When it is time for the dog to greet your guest, put them on the leash and calmly walk into the room.

Get the dog into a sitting position and keep rewarding them for remaining calm. Your guests can now approach and say, "Hello!" Stop the greeting and the rewards if your dog tries to jump. Refocus them and ask them to sit before carrying on with the greetings. Once your dog is calm and has greeted your guests. Give them more freedom on the leash to mingle.

Chapter 8:

Alright, Already!

What is worse? The sound of your neighbor's car alarm going off in the middle of the night or going into your third hour of listening to your dog whine. For me, it's the whining! Ignoring it doesn't work, shouting doesn't work, and as soon as you reward the behavior by showing them attention, they realize it works in their favor.

Dogs generally don't just bark or whine for fun. They are usually trying to communicate what they think is vital information to you. The problem is that our definition and their definition of "vital" may be very different, and most of the time, we really don't need to know that there is another dog walking down the street.

While the thought of having a silent dog sounds like bliss, it's very important to ensure that they don't stop communicating with us completely. In this chapter, we are going to work through some common causes and fixes. The goal is to teach your dog what information you need them to relay and what is of no use to either of you.

Why Is This Happening?

Dogs communicate through barking, whining, and moaning. They even have different barks to tell you different things. You need to learn your dog's noises and the body language that is paired with it to understand what they are trying to tell you. Some of it might be more important than you think!

I'm SO Happy to See You!

Barking is quite a normal greeting for dogs. It is especially common when greeting their favorite human friend. They have heard the way that the pitch of your voices changes when you are excited to see them. You get to say, "Hello! I missed you!" and they like to mimic your excitement and reply in the same way. The problem is that this barking can become excessive when they begin to greet everything, including their shadow, with high-pitched barks.

Excitement barks are usually paired with happy body language such as wagging the tail, perking up the ears, and jumping. In no way is this a negative behavior, and you should never punish it. It's simply bad manners, and you can teach them other ways to show you they missed you.

Isn't My Voice Beautiful?

Some dogs are more vocal than others. Breeds that are used to living in packs, such as Siberian Huskies and Malamutes, often communicate with each other through howling. They are highly sensitive to the communicative noises other dogs make and will typically respond with a nice big "Awwooo!"

Dogs that were bred or trained as security or guard dogs are on high alert all the time. Their job is to keep you safe and let you know if there is any suspicious activity happening around the house. There is not a drop of water from a leaky tap that can evade their detection. If they are unsure in any way, they will let you know by barking until you arrive at the scene. The key is to teach them what they are barking at is not actually a threat.

I'm SO Bored!

In case you missed it the last hundred times I said it, boredom is one of the biggest contributors to behavioral problems. Keep your dog busy! Dogs that don't have enough mental or physical stimulation will be packed with energy. Barking is a great way to release this energy. They may also bark at you to let you know that they are bored and frustrated.

Why Don't You Love Me?

Mom! Mom! Mom! Mom! I don't know about you, but when my dog does this while I am working, I close my eyes and pretend I'm asleep (or dead if I'm having a bad day). Sometimes it works; other times I get a paw in my mouth. If you shout at them, they are rewarded. They might even think you are trying to bark back! If you give them attention, they are rewarded. The next time you stop scratching them, you can expect a bark to get you started again. As annoying as this behavior is. You need to try to ignore it. Close your eyes and pretend you're asleep.

Attention seeking can also be a sign of separation anxiety. This is a big problem if your neighbors are less than understanding. If you struggle to get this behavior under control, you may need to look into using a doggy day care facility.

There Is Something Out There!

These are the barks you don't want to ignore. Most owners can tell when their dog is barking a warning. Their voices suddenly go low. Their bodies are rigid, the hairs on their back stand up, and their ears are flat. My body ends up doing the same thing, and I am tempted to push them through the door first to save me from the boogeyman, especially when it's late at night. You need to be the grownup here, pretend you're not scared, and investigate the situation. You don't have to respond to your dog, but you do need to respond to what they are barking at. If you find that the stimulus is not actually a threat, such as the mailman or the neighbor, you will need to work at desensitizing them.

You will need to correct this behavior as soon as possible, as the longer it continues, the more ingrained it will become. If your dog barks at your neighbor every morning when they walk to the car, they are rewarded when the neighbor gets into the car and leaves. Your dog has learned that the bark works, and they will continue to do it.

Help! I'm Scared!

Barking at a stimulus that is making them feel anxious or scared can be similar to warning barks. The body behavior will likely be slightly different and is usually accompanied by a tucked tail, shaking, and crouching. Whatever they are barking at, it is clearly quite frightening. These barks may not be directed at an object or person, it could just be a fear response to a thunderstorm or fireworks.

This kind of behavior needs to be corrected through desensitization and should never be rewarded. The more you reward the fear, the more fearful they will become!

Dogs that are suffering from vision or hearing impairment are also prone to fear barking. This may be a little more challenging, but there are changes you can make in your home to help them.

Please Keep Quiet!

Before we get into how to make it stop, you need to know what not to do!

Electronic collars, spray bottles, and rattle cans are a definite no-no. If your dog is barking out of fear, this is only going to make it much worse. A muzzle is not a cure for barking and is considered cruel if used for extended periods of time. Your dog won't be able to eat, drink, or pant.

Don't shout! This simply rewards the behavior as they have achieved their goal of getting your attention.

Don't encourage it. Saying, "What's that?" or howling back is encouraging the behavior. You need to be as consistent as possible when training.

Don't reward it! If your dog is barking for food, wait for them to stop before you give it to them. If they are barking to get out of their crate, patiently wait for them to stop before opening it up for them.

Now that we know what not to do, let's work at fixing it.

Curb the Boredom

I am so bored, I could scream! Bored dogs are going to find a way to get their energy out. Keep them as busy as you possibly can. Use interactive toys like snuffle mats, lick mats, treat dispensers, and food puzzles. Tired dogs aren't going to be interested in barking. Ensuring your dog has had enough exercise is a sure way to curb the barking behavior.

Remove the Motivation

Sometimes the easiest way to cure a fear response is to remove the source. If you live on a busy road, and your dog feels threatened by the amount of people walking past the house, close the curtains! If they bark when outdoors, go outside with them and play a game. Some dogs may even be triggered by silence. If this is the case, put on some background noise such as music or their favorite TV show. In my house, *The Lion King* works pretty well.

Desensitize

If you are unable to remove the source of the fear, you will need to desensitize your dog to it. This can take a while, but it is definitely worth it to provide your dog a comfortable and happy life. Desensitization works best if you use a clicker. If you have already trained your dog to respond to the clicker, you will need to start introducing the stimulus.

Your dog has a threshold. When they reach this threshold, they will emotionally react to the stimulus as they become fearful or stressed. When using desensitization training, you always want them below this threshold. If they are reacting to a specific loud noise, such as fireworks or thunder, you will want to introduce this noise very quietly.

Take your dog into a quiet, calm room and click and treat. When they have started to focus on you, begin playing the noise softly. You will notice that their ears will perk up. At this point, you want them to refocus on you! Click and treat when they look at you and continue until they feel confident again. You can now raise the volume a little more.

As soon as you see your dog is reaching their threshold, stop training! That is enough for them for the day. Continue it again tomorrow. As you work through this, you will find that your dog becomes less and less reactive to the noise.

Train an Incompatible Behavior

This works well if your dog barks when guests come over. Figure out what triggers the bark. Is it the doorbell? The gate opening? The sound of a car driving by? Bribe a friend to help by replicating the stimulus. A glass of wine may be needed. It can get a little boring!

Train your dog to produce any behavior that will distract them from the stimulus. This could be the command "toy," which would direct them to go play with their toys. "Place" or "bed" works well, and your dog should respond by going to their special place or bed.

Practice this until they are obeying your commands and producing the behavior you want. Then, introduce the stimulus. Get your friend to ring the doorbell and tell your dog the command "bed." If they obey, treat!

Repeat these steps until your dog is displaying this behavior by themselves. Continue to reward them when they exhibit this behavior, even without your command. Keep up the tasty rewards for the next few months.

Stop training if you can see your dog is becoming irritable. Slow and steady wins the race. You can continue tomorrow!

Extinction

Extinction works well for curbing attention barking. However, this training only works if you stay consistent. Stop reacting to the barking, and your dog will learn that it doesn't work.

Using extinction can often lead to extinction bursts, which can be incredibly frustrating. Dogs that demand bark for attention will begin to bark louder and more often in a last attempt of getting what they want from you. Once this peak has been hit, and you have managed to keep your cool and not give in to acknowledging it, your dog will stop.

Quiet Training

Train your dog to understand what the word "quiet" means. When they start barking at you, say the command in a calm, firm voice. When they stop barking, click and treat. Wait a few seconds to ensure there is no lingering bark in that throat before rewarding. They will start to figure out what you want from them, and the next time they bark, you can use the command to make them stop.

Put It on Cue

You can also put the barking behavior on cue. Teach your dog to speak. Encourage them to bark by saying, "Speak." You can do a little bark yourself if it helps to get them going. Click and treat the behavior when they do it on command. Do not reward when they do it without command.

You can now bounce between commanding them to speak and commanding them to be quiet. The most important thing here is to make sure that your commands and rewards are crystal clear! Wait a few seconds between using the next command.

Chapter 9:

Where Are the Brakes on This Thing?

There is nothing quite as fun as turning a relaxing afternoon walk into a sweat-inducing sprint, and the great part is if you start to get tired, your dog will drag you the rest of the way. All jokes aside, this is probably the most common behavioral problem that dog owners deal with, and it's exhausting. A lot of owners quickly give up and accept the fact that walking is no longer an option.

The issue is that they aren't able to keep up with the exercise routine their dog needs to stay fit and healthy. Playing catch in the yard can only do so much, and the dog becomes less and less desensitized to the outside world. Sometimes a little chubbier too! This, in itself, can lead to a ton of new difficulties.

The good news is you aren't the only one experiencing this, and over the years, trainers have come up with new, more effective training methods that can solve the trouble quickly. As with any undesirable behaviors, there is always a root cause. Figuring out that cause is key, as it enables you to decide which training method will work best.

Why Is This Happening?

This Hurts

Your dog is not going to want to walk if they are feeling miserable. Arthritis and injuries to the leg or paw are the most common health reasons, but even tummy aches and illnesses can affect them. Make sure your dog is feeling up for it. You shouldn't have to drag them out of the house.

Another factor that many owners don't take into account is how sensitive their little paw pads really are. When you head out for a walk on a hot day, put your hand down on the asphalt and check the temperature. If your hand burns, their paws are going to burn! You can seriously injure your dog by forcing them to walk on hot roads or sand. Opt for the park or a similar area so that they enjoy the cool grass.

If you can't avoid hot pavements or freezing cold snow, consider buying a set of booties. These are specially designed to protect your dog's feet and come in a variety of sizes and colors. This ensures a comfortable fit, and your dog can maintain their fashionista reputation.

Health Check

You can give your dog a brief health check at home. Sit calmly together and gently feel up and down each of your dog's legs. Start at the hip and work your way under their paws. Push gently on their joints and see if your dog reacts in any way. Pulling away from you, whimpering, or giving you a warning look is a clear sign that you have touched a sensitive spot. This could indicate a sprain or arthritis. If you suspect an injury, it's time for a trip to the vet!

This Is Not Comfortable at All...

Does your dog get the jiggles when you are walking? That means they are uncomfortable! Their harness is either too loose or too tight. If your leash is too long, it can wrap under their legs. Collars can also become quite annoying if you have connected your leash directly to it. If it's too tight, your dog is going to feel like they are choking. Loose collars will move around the dog's neck depending on how they move their heads. This constant friction can be very annoying, and you won't be able to direct your dog with as much control.

Choose the Right Equipment

The equipment you choose needs to fit comfortably and provide support. Make sure to select items that work for your dog's size and temperament. Without this, your walks will become a miserable affair.

Leashes and Leads

Every dog owner should own one leash and one lead.

A lead is a type of long leash which ranges anywhere between 20–100 feet long. It gives them the freedom to move away from you, but you still have control if they decide to run too far. This makes it a great tool for recall training.

Short leashes are awesome for walking and close contact training. This gives you more control over your dog as it keeps them at your side. It also allows you to softly pull back and stop walking when your dog is misbehaving. Using long leads for walking is guaranteed to end up with one of you flying through the air!

While I suggest you opt for a harness over a slip-leash. These do have their place. They can be used for reactive dogs and are much, much kinder than choke collars. Slip-leashes can be compared to lassos. The leash fits around the dog's neck and loops through a ring which sits comfortably on the back of the neck. If the dog pulls, the leash tightens, but as soon as they stop, the leash loosens back to a comfortable position.

Retractable leashes should be avoided during walks as it can teach your dog bad walking manners. These leashes apply a constant pressure, which the dog learns is normal. When using a normal leash, your dog will continue to pull to replicate the feeling.

Collars

Dogs should be comfortably fitted with flat collars on which you can clip their identification information. It's not recommended that you walk your dog with just a collar until you are completely confident that they are not going to dash off into the sunset.

Harness

Harnesses are highly recommended for walking reactive and untrained dogs. The harness allows you to have full control over your dog as it places pressure on the chest rather than the neck.

Front clip harnesses are a great option for dogs that pull, while back clip harnesses work well for comfortable walking and small dogs. You can purchase harnesses which offer both options. Some are even fitted with handles on the back. Handles come in handy if you are dealing with a reactive dog, as it gives you the option to hold them securely without having to pull back. If all else fails, you can even pick them up like a handbag.

Ill-fitting harnesses can cause chaffing, and your dog may struggle to breathe if it is too tight. Make sure that you fit it correctly and move your hand underneath the straps to ensure that there is enough space for your dog's chest to comfortably expand during exercise. Check how your harness fits before each walk and adjust it if your dog has gained or lost weight.

I Am So Glad You Like Running Too!

If you are rewarding your dog's pulling behavior by trying to keep up with them, they think they are doing the right thing. You must enjoy it if you're panting as much as they are, right? Be consistent in your training. If you want to go slower, you need to show them.

If you want to run with your dog, use a cue word like "run" to trigger the behavior and a cue word such as "heel" to end it. Choose your running phrase carefully and make sure it's not used in other training methods. If you use "let's go" for running and for getting in the car, you are going to end up having an awkward conversation with a very confused stranger that suddenly has a dog in their back seat.

This Place Is AMAZING!

Sensory overload! A dog's sense of smell is estimated to be around 10,000–100,000 times better than ours. Imagine the amount of information they are currently trying to process. Are you really that shocked that they suddenly stopped listening?

Allow Your Dog to Explore

Give your dog a chance to be a dog! There are so many new and exciting things around them, they can't help getting lost in their own nose. Give them a second to sniff around and process the new information. Take it slow, stay with them, and don't pull them back with force. If it's time to move, ask them to focus on you by giving them a command such as "sit." If they listen, treat and start your walk.

I Am Not Sure About This...

Dogs can get scared, and they are allowed to be apprehensive at times. If they haven't had the chance to get out into the world and experience different environments, it's only natural for them to be nervous on walks. If you are walking down residential roads, you may have neighbor dogs barking at you through the fence. It's an annoyance for you, but it is absolutely petrifying for them, and your dog may lunge at them or attempt to flee if they feel threatened.

If you have a chance to, change your route to a quieter one. If not, you will need to work on your dog's social skills to better prepare them for the outside world. We will discuss how to do this in-depth in the next chapter.

Come On, Let's Go!

If your dog is full of pent-up energy, it can be quite difficult to get them to slow down to your speed. I had a Greyhound that suddenly evolved into a rabbit when it was time to walk. If she couldn't go forward, she was at least going to go up! Prewalk playing used to help curb the excitement. They don't need to be exhausted before you get them walking, but they need to be calm.

Keep Calm and Walk On

Who let the dogs out? You! You! You! If you have an overly excitable dog that loves to bolt out the door the moment it opens, you have got a problem! Not only is this incredibly dangerous, but your dog is also getting the impression that they are in charge of the upcoming activity. This behavior needs to be corrected before you can even think of walking nicely.

Step One: Take Back the Power!

Harness up your pup, secure their leash, and get out that treat bag. Gather the leash up so that you have a firm grip and walk up to the door. By this point, your pup should be vibrating with excitement. Stand by the door and wait patiently. Eventually, your dog is going to turn around and look at you for direction. You need to ask them to sit.

Once their bum is on their ground, and their eyes are on you, give them a treat and tell them well done!

Step Two: All Eyes on Me!

Plant your feet firmly on the ground because now you are going to open the door. If they blast out, it's tough luck for them. Redirect them back inside, close the door, and start over. You want their bum on the floor and their eyes on you even after the door is open. Remember to reward your dog every time they sit and every time they look at you for direction.

Step Three: One Step at a Time

After a few repeats, you should be able to open the door without losing their attention. You can now walk outside. The same rule is going to apply here. If they try to run while you are walking out the door, you need to redirect them back inside and start from the beginning.

It's tedious, I know, but don't give in just yet. They will eventually understand what you want, and after a few tries, the two of you will be able to walk out that door calmly. This is not a once-off training session. You need to practice this behavior every single time you open that door.

Let's Get Walking

Now that your dog is not bursting out the door like an escaped convict, you can begin walk training. Start in your backyard or indoors if you have the space.

Step One: Use Your Leash

The way you are holding the leash is surprisingly important. If you have your dog walking on your left-hand side, you want to hold your leash firmly in your right hand. You will be using your left hand to pull the leash and direct your dog. When it's time to turn or redirect, slide your left hand down the leash to your knee. This provides enough horizontal tension and will gently pull your dog to where you want them to be. Hold this position until your turn is complete.

Step Two: Keep Their Attention

The world is jam-packed with new and exciting sights and smells, which makes you the most boring aspect of the walk. It is only natural for your dog's attention to drift off to something more rewarding. Walk forward, use your leash, and turn. All their attention is suddenly going to shift straight back to you. By being unpredictable, you can ensure that your dog will constantly keep you in mind and focus on what you are doing rather than what is around them.

Step Three: Ignore the Bad

When your dog begins to pull, stop walking and wait for them to redirect their attention back to you. When the leash is loose, and they are focusing on you, reward and keep walking.

Step Four: Reward the Good

Reward, reward, reward! When your dog successfully turns, give them a treat, a vocal reward, or even a toy! When they sit and look at you for direction, reward! When they are walking with a loose leash, reward! By rewarding all the good behavior, they will forget all about the negative behaviors that previously felt good.

Step Five: Up the Difficulty

Start to incorporate new distractions. This could be people walking down the street, cars driving past, or even ducks swimming in the local pond. It doesn't matter what you choose, just make sure you start at a distance.

Take it slow and walk calmly past the distraction. If the leash stays loose, reward them. If they start to focus on the distraction, redirect them by turning. The moment their focus is back on you, give them a reward!

If your dog has done well, walk past the distraction again, but this time, go a little closer. Only do this if you are absolutely sure you have your dog's full attention. Don't set them up for failure; you can try again tomorrow.

If only two ducks get to float away bark free, your dog has done well! Redirect them and walk back the way you came. Always celebrate the little wins.

Off-Leash Walking—Is It Okay?

Off-leash walking is the dream! You get to prowl around town with your pup in tow, no care in the world. As lovely as it seems, it is almost always a bad idea. Off-leash walking is only possible if you have a dog that is well-trained in recall. If your dog does not come running when you call their name, put that leash back on. If they do not obey recall, you can be assured that a time will come when they dash off after something unknown, and you will be sprinting after them screaming their name like a maniac. Some communities also have leash laws, so you'll want to abide by those as well.

Different dogs also have different social skills. Be aware that there are other people out there trying their best to train their dogs. If your pup decides to run up and give a reactive dog a sniff, there may be a fight. Not only does your dog stand a chance at being injured, you have also just ruined that other dog's training. "But my dog is friendly" is not a good enough excuse.

Don't be a buzzkill! If you are determined to walk off-leash, train your dog to obey recall and only remove the leash when undertaking isolated activities such as hiking.

Chapter 10:

Who Needs Friends Anyway?

If you are having problems socializing your dog, you are experiencing one of two things. Your dog seems terrified and desperately tries to flee the situation, or they go into complete attack mode and lunge at the nearest threatening target. Both of these, especially the latter, are likely to put you in a complete state of panic, as nobody wants to own an aggressive dog.

While it may seem easier to just stop taking your dog to the park or work out which times of the day your walking route is quietest, there will come a time when social situations are inevitable. These can quickly become dangerous as your dog will suddenly be stuck in a situation that they don't know how to handle, and their behavior can become unpredictable.

Getting your dog to socialize with other dogs can be a little tricky at first, but with time and patience, you can get it done. Even if it's just to teach an introverted dog that other pups are not as threatening as they may seem.

Is Your Dog Social?

Dogs may have been pack animals, but that doesn't necessarily mean that they are all happy in social situations. Just like us, dogs have their own personalities and preferences. There are certain things they enjoy and certain things they don't. When they meet a like-minded friend, they are sure to have a ball. However, that doesn't mean they will like everyone.

Social Dogs

Highly tolerant and social, dogs are more than happy to take a tail to the face if it means they get to play with someone else and have a great time. They are happy to meet new friends and quickly adapt to all types of play styles.

Tolerant Dogs

Dogs that have a midrange tolerance level are generally happier with a smaller group of friends. They know each other well enough to know how to play together and when to leave each other alone. They typically don't mind other dogs, but they can become irritable if approached by an excitable pup that doesn't know how to play by the rules.

Antisocial Dogs

Antisocial dogs do not play well with others. They will often become aggressive when approached and are much happier left alone.

Aggressive, antisocial dogs are a product of previous trauma or a lack of socialization as a puppy. If they have been in a traumatic situation with another dog, they are likely to bite first and ask questions later in an attempt to keep themselves safe.

Dogs that were not socialized as puppies are typically antisocial because they are scared. They don't quite know how to deal with an unexpected lick from a stranger.

Introverts

Yes, there are introverted dogs, and no, they aren't necessarily aggressive. These pups likely received the right amount of socialization when young but have simply decided that they prefer humans. Introverts are usually tolerant of other dogs, and while happy to go to the park for a walk or game of catch, they are not too interested in playing with anyone else.

There is nothing wrong with this behavior. If your dog is happy and healthy and displays no aggression toward others, don't force them into social situations. Sometimes it's okay to not have any friends.

Understanding Body Language

Understanding your dog's body language is going to be the difference between a fun-loving greeting and World War III. By knowing how they feel, you will be able to judge the situation better and decide whether to continue with the introduction or raise your white flag and call it a day.

Posture

It's generally quite easy to gauge how a dog feels based on their posture. A relaxed body is a good body. If they put their chest on the ground and bum in the air, they are ready to play!

When your dog is feeling upset, you can actually see their muscles tense up. If they are cowering or hunched to the ground, they are definitely not feeling comfortable. They do this to make themselves as small as possible to indicate that they are not a threat.

If they go straight into the attack pose with their weight shifted forward and their heads lowered, you have got a problem, especially if this is accompanied by snarls and intense staring. This is equivalent to saying, "Come at me, bro!" If the intended target does not back down, you can expect your dog to lunge.

If you see that the hair on their back is standing up, it means that they are incredibly intrigued by whatever is in front of them. It's exactly the same as us getting goose bumps! This is not necessarily a negative behavior, but if it is accompanied by barking, growling, or negative posture, it can indicate a threat.

The Way of the Wag

Wagging tails aren't always a sign of happiness. They are just a way for your dog to display an emotional response. Long, sweeping wags that jiggle their whole bodies are the best kind of wags. This means that they are happy and excited to see you.

If your dog's tail is up and twitching quickly, proceed with caution. This doesn't necessarily mean aggression, but it does mean that they are having a strong emotional response to the stimuli in front of them. The higher your dog's tail is, the most assertive and confident they are. If this is accompanied by other negative body language, it is a sign of aggression.

Low hanging tails, especially ones that are tucked in between their legs, are a sign of fear or submission. This is not a happy tail and most certainly not a happy dog. Retreat and do something they enjoy to distract them.

What Are You Doing With Your Mouth?

Snarling is the most obvious signal your dog can make with their mouth, and you already know that it means trouble. If this is accompanied by growls, it's time to retreat. Dogs do also smile. While this may seem similar to a snarl, their mouths are generally much more relaxed. This is their way of letting you know they are friendly.

Snarls and smiles are not the only way your dog communicates. If you find that they are yawning a lot, they could be feeling stressed out. This is often accompanied by lip licking and excessive swallowing.

If Looks Could Kill

If your dog turns their head and avoids eye contact at all costs, it means they are stressed or feeling uncomfortable. They will typically try to flee the situation, or if your dog is anything like mine, they will hide between your legs and ask you to sort out the bully.

On the opposite end of the spectrum, if your dog is staring daggers at another, they are trying to threaten them. If you are struggling to snap them out of it, you should remove them from the situation immediately. They are clearly too focused on the other dog to obey you.

Let's Get Sniffing

Before you start training, you need to figure out what you actually want to achieve and set yourself some goals. In this chapter, we are going to work on the following:

- keeping your dog calm when visiting a new area

- being able to walk without your dog reacting to other dogs or people on the road

- stopping your dog from trying to eat your guests

- helping your dog make a new friend

These seem pretty simple, but they are going to be the foundational steps to proper socialization.

Goal One: Keep Calm

If your dog does not feel comfortable walking in a new environment without people and dogs around, you cannot expect them to feel comfortable in the park! Dogs that have been isolated will often become incredibly anxious when faced with too many new things all at once. Start with the basics and avoid placing them in the middle of a terrifying situation.

If your dog is comfortable in your backyard, start there! Use this space to practice your command, walking, and recall training. Start introducing random items from the strange outside world that your dog hasn't been exposed to. This could include anything from plants to your dirty shoes and blankets that smell of other dogs.

Now, work your way out. Does your dog get nervous when the two of you are in the front yard? Then stop there. Turn this into a fun experience by playing a game. Reward confident behavior, and they will soon learn that this is not as scary as it may seem.

It's all about flipping their perspective. You want to change something they fear into an opportunity to get a reward or play a fun game. When they are a little more confident, walk out your gate.

It is so important to remember to keep your dog below their response threshold. If they stop accepting treats or responding to you, they are overloaded. It's time to go home and relax.

Goal Two: Stop Reacting

Now that your pup understands that the world outside your gate is not, in fact, an alien planet, you can begin working on desensitizing them to people and other dogs. Remember, they are not reacting negatively to strangers because it's fun; it's because they are frightened.

You may find that they react to certain people. If they have only been exposed to women, they will be understandably nervous of much larger, taller men. If they have never been exposed to children, they are probably trying to figure out what kind of strange, furless dog is in front of them.

Thankfully, the streets are full of people of different ages, sexes, sizes, and clothing preferences. Find a quiet spot where you can maintain at least a 20-foot distance from a frequently walked path or road. If your dog is still feeling uneasy, you can move a little further away.

Use their absolute favorite treats for this activity. If they love sausages, stock up on sausages! Every time they look at a person walking past, use your clicker and reward them. Stop rewarding when the person has walked out of view. Once they feel more comfortable, you can move closer to the road and start again. If your dog becomes reactive, redirect them and return to the 20-foot mark to start again. If they become unresponsive to the rewards, they are too overwhelmed. Call it a day and go home to relax.

You are going to be using the same steps to desensitize your dog to other pups. I suggest walking around a dog park first. Keep a reasonable distance so that your dog is not overwhelmed. You just want them to pick up on some smells and sounds. When the park is quiet, you can walk your dog along the fence line and give them a chance to sniff around.

When they begin to relax around the area, you can work on getting them a little closer. For this, I recommend finding a cooperative owner with a calm, well-socialized dog. Get them to sit calmly 20 feet away from you. Every time your dog notices them, you can click and reward. You can start to walk closer as your pup feels more comfortable, but remember, this is not an introduction! Redirect your dog before you get too close.

Repeat these steps at a 20-foot distance while the other dog is performing different activities. Ask them to walk past, play a game or make some noises. If at any point your dog is feeling uncomfortable, redirect them away from the situation and start again at a further distance.

Goal Three: Please Don't Eat My Friends

Assuming you achieved goal number two, and your dog is no longer reacting to strangers, you can start to let those strangers into your home. Please don't get real strangers, just friends of yours that your dog hasn't met yet!

I like to start the introduction by bringing home some of my friend's clothes for my dog to sniff. They gain a lot of valuable information from this, and they won't need to sniff as hard when my guests arrive. Choose a mutual setting that your dog can enter and exit at all times. They need to feel as though they can escape the situation without having to pull the fire alarm. A backyard or living room works well.

Place your dog in their crate or behind a baby gate until your guests are settled. When are you sure your dog is calm, open up and allow them to enter or exit the room. Continue your conversation as you normally would.

Do not get your guests to approach your dog first or get them to give your dog treats out of their hands. You want your dog to make the first move. If they decide to stay hidden, you can ask your guests to throw them a couple of treats to prove that they are friendly.

At the end of the day, if your dog decides not to come and greet your friends, that is fine too! There was no negative behavior, your dog learned some valuable information, and they will likely be much braver the next time around.

The same method can be used for a reactive dog, but you will need to ensure your guest's safety. Keep your dog on a leash at all times, and if you notice they are becoming anxious, remove them from the situation.

Goal Four: Making Some New Friends

If your dog has achieved the first three goals with flying colors, you can now attempt a dog-on-dog greeting! Find a friend or family member who has a calm, well-socialized dog and organize a doggy play date. It's best to meet on mutual ground, and a quiet park with no other distractions works well.

Keep both dogs on loose leashes and get confident. Your dog can sense when you are anxious. When you see your friend, you can begin to approach each other slowly. Chat as you normally would to keep yourself and your dog from getting tense.

When you eventually meet up, allow the two dogs to sniff each other calmly. Dogs' greetings are short and sweet. They don't need to spend an hour having a conversation over coffee. A five-minute sniff to size the other one up is more than enough. Once this time is up, redirect your dog a few paces and play a game to reward them.

If it all goes well, you can walk up for another greeting a little later. Repeat this a few times a week, extending the greeting period by a few minutes each time.

Keep an eye on your dog's behavior during the interaction. If you see that they are becoming at all jittery, redirect them a few paces back and play a game while the other dog is still in sight. You need to show your pup that they are not a threat before attempting another introduction.

Before you try this out, ask yourself, does your dog really need a friend, and is it worth a potentially bad experience to get them one? If your dog is still reactive and aggressive to other dogs that come near, stop trying. Sometimes the trauma goes a little too deep, and if you have managed to get your pup walking calmly with you, that is enough.

Professional behaviorists and dog trainers are great options in situations like this, especially if you find that you are becoming increasingly anxious. They have the knowledge and experience to calmly handle socialization scenarios and will be able to offer hands-on assistance.

For more serious cases, consider giving your dog calming medications before you begin your training. If you have chosen this route, be sure to work closely with both your veterinarian and trainer to ensure that your dog is getting the best possible care.

The most important thing to remember is not to push their boundaries. Keep working at getting them to feel safe and confident. Who knows? In a couple of months, they may be ready.

Conclusion

Time flies when you're having fun, right? Don't worry! Even though the book is finished, your journey with your best pal has only just begun.

If I have done my job right, you should be feeling calmer and much more optimistic about the future. You have been armed with up-to-date training techniques and behavioral correction methods. You should be bursting with confidence and prepared to share your expertise with your friends, family, and that one neighbor whose dog enjoys barking for hours on end, unless you are watching your dog chew up the couch right now... What a mood killer!

If that's the case, I would just like to remind you that everything is going to be okay! There will be good days and bad days, but it is important to remember that consistency and patience are key. Don't give up on your dog, because they sure won't be giving up on you. Take a deep breath and work through the steps. Watching your dog change and flourish will be the greatest reward you can imagine.

This is not a one-man job. You will need to work with your dog to figure out the best way forward. If you take the time to listen to them, they will tell you exactly what they like and don't like. If you find that some of these methods aren't quite working for you and your pup, don't be afraid to switch it up and innovate! Small adjustments can lead to huge changes.

This book should be used as your reference guide. When you are feeling unsure, scroll back to the chapter you need. Bookmark the chapters that apply to you the most, scribble in your notes, and read it to your dog! Do whatever you need to do to get the most out of the information I have provided.

On the worst days, when you feel like you just can't do it anymore, seek out a friend. There are tons of support groups out there for owners of aggressive and reactive dogs. If this is something that you are struggling with, I highly recommend that you look into joining a local group or one of the many online ones. Having the chance to talk to somebody else who is working through the same problems as you can be a lifesaver.

It's now time to pick yourself up, give your pup a big kiss and head to the local pet store to gear up for your adventure! Pick out a great harness and leash, grab some fun toys, and don't forget your pup's favorite treats.

If you have enjoyed this book, please leave a review on Amazon.

About the Author

I can't remember a time in my life when I was not completely obsessed with dogs! Especially the ones that nobody else wants. Growing up, I had to constantly resist the urge to bring home every stray puppy I saw, and each time, my heart broke a little more. When the opportunity finally arose for me to provide one of these lost souls with the perfect home, I drove straight to the shelter.

However, I soon found myself overwhelmed by all the problems that come with rescuing a dog, so I set out to learn the best way to train and heal my new soulmate. Inspired by my favorite behaviorists and dog trainers, I decided to follow in their footsteps and help as many people and pups as possible.

For the last 30 years, I have dedicated my time to studying different training techniques—the good, the bad, and the ugly—and I came to learn exactly which ones produced the results I wanted. The end goal is not just a trained dog. The goal is a well-adjusted, healthy, and happy dog that obeys your commands out of respect and love, not fear!

My books are compiled of tried-and-true techniques that have personally helped me to work with my dogs and provide them the best life that I can.

Remember! It's all about working with your dog, not getting your dog to work for you.

—Hope Chambers

References

AKC Staff. (2019, September 26). AKC groups: Sporting, hound, working, terrier, toy, non-sporting, Herding. *American Kennel Club*. https://www.akc.org/expert-advice/lifestyle/7-akc-dog-breed-groups-explained/

All Dogs Unleashed. (2019, August 1). Teaching a hunting dog not to chase - The challenges of training hounds with strong instincts. *All Dogs Unleashed Dallas*. https://www.alldogsunleashed.com/blog/training-hounds-with-strong-instincts/

Anderson, E. (2021, January 20). Punishment vs. interruption: Properly managing your dog's behavior. *Whole Dog Journal*. https://www.whole-dog-journal.com/behavior/punishment-vs-interruption-properly-managing-your-dogs-behavior/

Asher, M. (2020, February 20). Dog training methods and 5 essential dog obedience commands. *Pets Best*. https://www.petsbest.com/blog/dog-training-basic-commands/

Ashley, S. A. (2020, April 6). Dog body language: 45 ways your dog is secretly communicating with you. *PureWow*. https://www.purewow.com/family/dog-body-language

ASPCA. (n.d.). Behavioral help for your pet. *ASPCA*. https://www.aspca.org/pet-care/general-pet-care/behavioral-help-your-pet

ASPCA. (2014, September 25). House training your dog or puppy. *ASPCA*. https://www.aspca.org/news/house-training-your-dog-or-puppy

ASPCA. (2015). Common dog behavior issues. *ASPCA.* https://www.aspca.org/pet-care/dog-care/common-dog-behavior-issues

Australia, B. P. (n.d.). Tired of yapping? How to stop nuisance dog barking. *Buddy Pet Australia.* https://buddypet.co/blogs/learn/tired-of-yapping-how-to-stop-nuisance-dog-barking

Battersea. (2020, February 21). How to teach your dog not to jump up. *Battersea.* https://www.battersea.org.uk/pet-advice/dog-advice/how-teach-your-dog-not-jump

Becker, M. (2022, September 21). Dog training 101: Essential tools you'll need. *Vetstreet.* https://www.vetstreet.com/our-pet-experts/dog-training-101-essential-tools-youll-need

Bender, A. (2020, May 6). Training small dogs: What you need to know. *The Spruce Pets.* https://www.thesprucepets.com/tips-for-training-small-dog-breeds-1118254

Bender, A. (2021a, February 5). Teach an old dog new tricks: 5 training tips. *The Spruce Pets.* https://www.thesprucepets.com/training-tips-for-adult-dogs-1118253

Bender, A. (2021b, February 13). Top 10 basic dog training commands. *The Spruce Pets.* https://www.thesprucepets.com/basic-dog-training-commands-1117311

Bennink, B. (n.d.). There is no such thing as a bad dog - Only untrained dogs. *Good Doggy.* https://www.gooddoggysaratoga.com/blog/2017/8/8/there-is-no-such-thing-as-a-bad-dogs-only-untrained-dogs

Blake, M. (2019, June 11). Guide to sporting dog breeds and characteristics. *LoveToKnow.* https://www.lovetoknowpets.com/dogs/sporting-dogs

Callahan, K. (2022, March 22). No need for force: How to stop your dog from pulling on leash and more. *Whole Dog Journal.* https://www.whole-dog-journal.com/training/how-to-stop-your-dog-from-pulling-on-the-leash/

Camps, T., Amat, M., & Manteca, X. (2019). A review of medical conditions and behavioral problems in dogs and cats. *Animals, 9(12), 1133.* https://doi.org/10.3390/ani9121133

Canine Scholars. (n.d.). Dog & puppy systematic desensitization training. *Canine Scholars Dog Training.* https://www.caninescholars.com/dog-training-methods/systematic-desensitization/

Chewy Editorial. (2016, December 20). 4 outdated dog training techniques to avoid. *BeChewy.* https://be.chewy.com/training-training-tips-5-outdated-dog-training-techniques-to-avoid/

Chewy Editorial. (2019, November 15). How to socialize an older dog: Expert trainer tips. *BeChewy.* https://be.chewy.com/socializing-an-older-dog/

Chewy Editorial. (2020, January 12). How to potty train an older dog. *BeChewy.* https://be.chewy.com/how-to-potty-train-an-older-dog/

Clason, D. (2022a, August 12). Follow these steps to successfully crate train your older dog. *PawTracks.* https://www.pawtracks.com/dogs/crate-train-older-dog/

Clason, D. (2022b, November 15). Steps you can take to stop the bad behavior of leash pulling. *PawTracks.* https://www.pawtracks.com/dogs/leash-pulling-training/

Crittenden, C. (2021, October 25). 5 basic commands every dog should know (and how to teach them). *Petful.* https://www.petful.com/behaviors/basic-commands-your-dog-should-know/

Culp, C. (2018, December 2). DOG PSYCHOLOGY Part 1: What is dog psychology? *Thriving Canine.* https://www.thrivingcanine.com/blog/2018/12/02/dog-psychology-part-1-what-dog-psychology

DeSantis, D. (2022, May 1). 21 dog training commands - basic to advanced for a well-behaved dog. *Puppy in Training.* https://puppyintraining.com/dog-training-commands/

Dog Academy. (2022, March 12). How to train a herding dog. *Dog Academy.* https://dogacademy.org/blog/herding-dog-training/

Dog Psychology 101. (2018, January 24). Dog psychology vs human psychology, dog psychology 101. *Dog Psychology 101.* https://dogpsychology101.com/human-psychology-vs-dog-psychology/

Dog Trust. (n.d.). How to stop your dog pulling on the lead. *Dog Trust.* https://www.dogstrust.org.uk/dog-advice/training/outdoors/walking-nicely-training

Dogtopia. (2019, February 11). How to socialize an older dog. *Dogtopia.* https://www.dogtopia.com/blog/how-to-socialize-an-older-dog/

Dugatkin, L. A. (2014). *Principles of Animal Behavior.* W.W. Norton & Company.

Dwilson, S. (2020, March 4). Is it too late to train my older dog? *K&H Pet Products.* https://khpet.com/blogs/dogs/how-late-is-too-late-to-train-an-older-dog

Eckstein, S. (2021, May 8). Understanding why dogs bark. *Fetch.* https://pets.webmd.com/dogs/guide/understanding-why-dogs-bark

Elliot, P. (2021, January 8). How to obedience train an older dog. *Wag Walking.* https://wagwalking.com/training/obedience-train-an-older-dog

Elliott, G. (2022, October 4). Kids and pets: What you need to know for safe interactions. *The Dog People.* https://www.rover.com/blog/introducing-a-dog-to-your-children/

Erb, H. (2020, December 1). How to potty train an older dog: Housetraining adult dogs. *American Kennel Club.* https://www.akc.org/expert-advice/training/how-to-housetrain-an-adult-dog/#:~:text=Take%20her%20out%20first%20thing

Farricelli, A. (2022, April 20). Can you really train a hound? *PetHelpful.* https://pethelpful.com/dogs/-Can-You-Really-Train-a-Hound

Fetch Masters. (n.d.). *Dog socialization problems. FetchMasters.* https://fetchmasters.com/dog-socialization-problems/

Feyrecilde, M., Horwitz, D., & Landsberg, G. (n.d.). Controlling pulling on walks. *VCA Animal Hospitals.* https://vcahospitals.com/know-your-pet/controlling-pulling-on-walks

Flowers, A. (2021, July 19). Dog behavioral problems - barking, chewing, and more. *Fetch.* https://pets.webmd.com/dogs/ss/slideshow-behaviorial-problems-in-dogs

Fulcher, S. (2014, January 2). Ten reasons your dog may develop behavior problems. *Clicker Training.* https://www.clickertraining.com/ten-reasons-your-dog-may-develop-behavior-problems

Gibeault, S. (2018, April 30). Positive rewards dog training tips. *American Kennel Club.* https://www.akc.org/expert-advice/training/training-rewards/

Gibeault, S. (2020a, January 27). Understanding dog body language: Decipher dogs' signs & signals. *American Kennel Club.* https://www.akc.org/expert-advice/advice/how-to-read-dog-body-language/#:~:text=Dogs%20with%20their%20tails%20pointing

Gibeault, S. (2020b, November 2). Changing your dog's behavior with desensitization & counterconditioning. *American Kennel Club.* https://www.akc.org/expert-advice/training/changing-your-dogs-behavior-with-desensitization-and-counter-conditioning/

Gibeault, S. (2020c, December 17). How to teach your dog to drop it. *American Kennel Club.* https://www.akc.org/expert-advice/training/teaching-your-dog-to-drop-it/#:~:text=Place%20a%20high%2Dvalue%20treat

Gibeault, S. (2020d, December 23). How to stop your dog from jumping up on people. *American Kennel Club.* https://www.akc.org/expert-advice/training/how-to-stop-your-dog-from-jumping-up-on-people/

Gibeault, S. (2021a, January 3). How to teach your dog to stay. *American Kennel Club.* https://www.akc.org/expert-advice/training/dont-move-fido-teach-your-dog-to-stay/

Gibeault, S. (2021b, February 3). How to teach your dog to sit. *American Kennel Club.* https://www.akc.org/expert-advice/training/how-to-teach-your-dog-to-sit/

Grayson, A. (2019, May 5). Not every dog is a social butterfly. *Augusta Grayson.* https://www.caninetraining.co.nz/blog/dog-dog-sociability

Green, S. (n.d.). Consequences that can come from a poorly trained dog. *Mummy Matters.* https://deepinmummymatters.com/consequences-can-come-poorly-trained-dog/

Hastings Staff. (2018, September 21). 8 ways to prepare your home for a new dog's arrival. *Hastings Veterinary Hospital*. https://hastingsvet.com/8-ways-to-prepare-your-home-for-a-new-dogs-arrival/

Hinds, J. (2016, December 14). 10 reasons why dogs pull. *Jo Hinds*. https://johinds.com/2016/12/14/8-reasons-why-your-dog-may-pull-on-the-lead/

Horowitz, A. (2022, November 11). 9 best dog training tools & products professional trainers swear By. *Pupford*. https://pupford.com/best-dog-training-products/

Horwitz, D. (n.d.-a). Dog behavior problems - greeting behavior - jumping up. *VCA*. https://vcahospitals.com/know-your-pet/dog-behavior-problems-greeting-behavior-jumping-up#:~:text=Usually%20the%20motivation%20for%20the

Horwitz, D. (n.d.-b). Overcoming fears with desensitization and counterconditioning. *VCA Animal Hospitals*. https://vcahospitals.com/know-your-pet/overcoming-fears-with-desensitization-and-counterconditioning#:~:text=Desensitization%20is%20a%20technique%20of

Hospital, L. V. V. (2020, November 13). Undoing the damage: untraining bad habits in dogs. *Leon Valley Veterinary Hospital*. https://www.leonvalleyvet.com/blog/undoing-damage-untraining-bad-habits-dogs/

Ingersoll, C. (n.d.). Is it ever too late to train a dog? *Alpha-Dog*. https://alphadogpets.com/blog/41578/is-it-ever-too-late-to-train-a-dog

Jones, J. (2022, November 28). Small dog training: How, where, when and why. *Small Dog Place*. https://www.smalldogplace.com/small-dog-training.html

Jones, O. (2021, October 15). Why do dogs jump on you? 3 reasons (and how to stop it). *Pet Keen*. https://petkeen.com/reasons-why-dogs-jump-on-people/

Kasinger, C. (2019, January 10). 8 tips to socialise your dog with other dogs and humans. *The Dog People*. https://www.rover.com/uk/blog/8-tips-to-socialise-your-dog-with-other-dogs-and-humans/

Kerns, N. (2011, March 1). (Proper greetings #3) Stop your dog from jumping on people. *Whole Dog Journal*. https://www.whole-dog-journal.com/tips/proper-greetings-3-stop-your-dog-from-jumping-on-people/

Kokocińska-Kusiak, A., Woszczyło, M., Zybala, M., Maciocha, J., Barłowska, K., & Dzięcioł, M. (2021). Canine olfaction: physiology, behavior, and possibilities for practical applications. *Animals, 11(8), 2463.* https://doi.org/10.3390/ani11082463

Kristen. (2014, September 7). Types of rewards - Miami dog training. *Crown Dog Training*. https://crowndogtraining.com/2014/09/07/types-of-rewards/

Landsberg, G. (2019). Behavioral problems of dogs. *Veterinary Manual; MSD Veterinary Manual.* https://www.msdvetmanual.com/behavior/normal-social-behavior-and-behavioral-problems-of-domestic-animals/behavioral-problems-of-dogs

Lange, K. E. (2022, June 10). From trauma to trust. *The Humane Society of the United States.* https://www.humanesociety.org/trauma-trust

Lawlor, V. (2021, December 17). How to potty train an older dog who's set in their ways. *PawTracks*. https://www.pawtracks.com/dogs/potty-training-an-older-dog/

Leonhardt, C. (2020, April 5). Dog training tools to avoid. *Busy Dog*. https://www.busydogcolorado.com/post/training-tools-to-avoid

Lesser, J. (2022, November 1). The 7 types of dog breeds. *The Spruce Pets*. https://www.thesprucepets.com/types-of-dog-breeds-4688776

London, K. B. (2022, May 16). A guide to dog-to-dog greetings. *The Wildest*. https://www.thewildest.com/dog-behavior/guide-dog-dog-greetings#:~:text=John%20Bradshaw%2C%20PhD%2C%20males%20typically

Long, E. (2022, October 31). How you "parent" your dog matters, actually. *Lifehacker*. https://lifehacker.com/how-you-parent-your-dog-matters-actually-1849721051

Lounge, H. (2021, June 28). How to socialize an adult dog and why it's never too late. *Hounds Lounge*. https://www.houndslounge.com/blog/how-to-socialize-an-adult-dog-and-why-its-never-too-late/#:~:text=It

Lowrey, S. (2022, March 11). Excessive dog barking: Reasons & and how to stop it. *American Kennel Club*. https://www.akc.org/expert-advice/training/excessive-dog-barking-causes-stop/

Lumontod, P. (2020, July 30). 25 most common dog behavior problems. *Top Dog Tips*. https://topdogtips.com/most-common-dog-behavior-problems/

Lunchick, P. (2018, September 25). Teach your puppy these 5 basic commands. *American Kennel Club*. https://www.akc.org/expert-advice/training/teach-your-puppy-these-5-basic-commands/

Madson, C. (2019a, January 29). Dog training aversives: What are they and why should you avoid them? *Preventive Vet*. https://www.preventivevet.com/dogs/dog-training-aversives

Madson, C. (2019b, February 27). How to help a dog that's missed early socialization. *Preventive Vet*. https://www.preventivevet.com/dogs/how-to-help-adult-dog-with-socialization

Madson, C. (2019c, March 26). How to stop your dog from door dashing. *Preventive Vet*. https://www.preventivevet.com/dogs/how-to-stop-your-dog-from-door-dashing

Madson, C. (2020a, August 25). Teaching your dog to stop jumping. *Preventive Vet*. https://www.preventivevet.com/dogs/stop-your-dog-from-jumping

Madson, C. (2020b, September 26). How to potty train an adult dog. *Preventive Vet*. https://www.preventivevet.com/dogs/how-to-potty-train-an-adult-dog

Madson, C. (2021, March 1). Does ignoring your dog's bad behavior work? *Preventive Vet*. https://www.preventivevet.com/dogs/ignoring-bad-behavior-in-dogs

Maev. (2020, July 7). How changing your dog's food can correct their behavioral issues. *Medium*. https://medium.com/@Maev/how-changing-your-dogs-food-can-correct-their-behavioral-issues-954831450326

Marrs, M. (2022, October 18). 8 essential dog training equipment items for 2022! *K9 of Mine*. https://www.k9ofmine.com/dog-training-equipment/

Martin, N. (2020, March 6). *How to Choose the Right Dog Crate: Your Complete Guide*. *The Dog People*. https://www.rover.com/blog/how-to-choose-right-dog-crate-complete-guide/

McCann Dog Training. (2019a). Are you accidentally being a BAD leader for your dog? [Video]. *YouTube.* https://www.youtube.com/watch?v=QntS570VFZ0&list=PL7 BBgLulhernWIrrSY_UWNauNDBssvmTi

McCann Dog Training. (2019b). The unpopular truth about socializing your dog [Video]. *YouTube.* https://www.youtube.com/watch?v=YVvd8RrRjRA

McCann Dog Training. (2021a). The 3 steps for teaching your dog to greet people nicely [Video]. *YouTube.* https://www.youtube.com/watch?v=BTlrYgOVbzY

McCann Dog Training. (2021b). Leash walking training for dogs that are ALWAYS pulling! [Video]. *YouTube.* https://www.youtube.com/watch?v=y2yj2xtCo-k

McCann Dog Training. (2021c). The BIG mistake people make when teaching a dog to drop something [Video]. *YouTube.* https://www.youtube.com/watch?v=IhHpc3MziLI/

McCann Dog Training. (2021d). STOP dog jumping IMMEDIATELY with a DIFFERENT approach! [Video]. *YouTube.* https://www.youtube.com/watch?v=zGNSSh7LOKc

McCann Dog Training. (2022a). STOP your dog from pulling on leash with this STRANGE game [Video]. *YouTube.* https://www.youtube.com/watch?v=PYcKKBWcg1o

McCann Dog Training. (2022b). Stop your dog from whining in their crate [Video]. *YouTube.* https://www.youtube.com/watch?v=wQq7PfXyQvY&t=533s

McMillan, B. (2022, October 26). Brandon McMillan's 10 essential dog training tools. *MasterClass.* https://www.masterclass.com/articles/brandon-mcmillans-essential-dog-training-tools

Meyers, H. (2021, January 11). Correcting dog behavior: How to stop bad dog behavior. *American Kennel Club*. https://www.akc.org/expert-advice/training/how-to-curb-unwanted-dog-behaviors/

Michaels, L. (2014, August 12). Pet parenting positively. *Dog Psychologist on Call*. https://www.dogpsychologistoncall.com/positive-pet-parenting/

Millan, C. (2015, June 18). How to crate train an adult dog. *Cesar's Way*. https://www.cesarsway.com/how-to-crate-train-an-adult-dog/

Millan, C. (2019a, September 25). How to socialize an adult dog. *Cesar's Way*. https://www.cesarsway.com/how-to-socialize-an-adult-dog/

Millan, C. (2019b, October 31). 5 essential commands you can teach your dog. *Cesar's Way*. https://www.cesarsway.com/5-essential-commands-you-can-teach-your-dog/

Nicholas, J. (2021, May 2). Everything you need to know about crate training your puppy or adult dog. *Preventive Vet*. https://www.preventivevet.com/dogs/everything-you-need-to-know-about-crate-training-your-puppy-or-adult-dog

Pachel, C. (2021, June 3). How to introduce a puppy or adult dog to your children. *Preventive Vet*. https://www.preventivevet.com/dogs/how-to-introduce-a-puppy-or-adult-dog-to-your-children

Palika, L. (2017, August 9). Dog behavior: My dog pulls on the leash. *Fear Free Happy Homes*. https://www.fearfreehappyhomes.com/dog-behavior-my-dog-pulls-on-the-leash/

Paretts, S. (2021, November 12). What to look for when choosing a dog crate. *American Kennel Club*. https://www.akc.org/expert-advice/training/what-to-look-for-when-choosing-a-dog-crate/#:~:text=Size%20is%20the%20most%20important

Parrish, C. (2022, November 17). Buying guide: How to choose the best dog crate for your pet. *BeChewy*. https://be.chewy.com/dog-crate-buying-guide/

PAWS. (n.d.). Re-housetraining your adult dog. *PAWS*. https://www.paws.org/resources/re-housetraining-your-adult-dog/

Paws Abilities. (2017, February 16). Understanding dog-dog sociability. *Paws Abilities*. https://paws4udogs.wordpress.com/2017/02/16/understanding-dog-dog-sociability/

Pet Backer. (2022, October). Are dogs social animals? *Pet Backer*. https://www.petbacker.com/blog/facts/are-dogs-social-animals

Pet Finder. (n.d.). Tips for the first 30 days of dog adoption. *Petfinder*. https://www.petfinder.com/dogs/bringing-a-dog-home/tips-for-first-30-days-dog/

Petmate Academy. (2020, November 12). 10 basic commands to teach your dog. *Petmate*. https://www.petmate.com/10-basic-commands-to-teach-your-dog/article/a90090

PetMD Editorial. (2014, June 13). How your dog's food affects his mood. *PetMD*. https://www.petmd.com/dog/centers/nutrition/evr_multi_how_your_dogs_food_affects_his_mood

PetMD Editorial. (2017, September 29). 5 reasons your dog won't stop barking. *PetMD*. https://www.petmd.com/dog/behavior/5-reasons-your-dog-wont-stop-barking

PetMD Editorial. (2018, February 6). How to heal an emotionally traumatized pet. *PetMD*. https://www.petmd.com/dog/behavior/how-heal-emotionally-traumatized-pet

Phenix, A. P. (2017, August 3). 5 training tips for your working dog breed. *Dogster*. https://www.dogster.com/dog-training/training-tips-for-your-working-dog-breed

Pryor, K. (2012, September 5). The eight ways of changing behavior. *Clicker Training*. https://www.clickertraining.com/node/290

Pryor, K. (2018). Don't shoot the dog! The new art of teaching and training. Ringpress Books Ltd.

Pyror, K. (2013, February 1). Don't socialize the dog! *Clicker Training*. https://www.clickertraining.com/dont-socialize-the-dog

Ramos, B. (2015, September 24). If your dog has these bad behaviors, you need to take them to obedience training. *SheKnows*. https://www.sheknows.com/living/articles/1094999/signs-your-dog-needs-obedience-training/

Randall, B. (2022, April 3). How to stop a dog pulling on the lead and start walking to heel. *Country Life*. https://www.countrylife.co.uk/out-and-about/dogs/how-to-stop-a-dog-pulling-on-the-lead-and-start-walking-to-heel-six-tips-from-top-dog-trainer-ben-randall-241134

Richmond, M. (2018, October 17). Five steps to stopping unwanted behavior. *Whole Dog Journal*. https://www.whole-dog-journal.com/training/five-steps-to-stopping-unwanted-behavior/

Robert Cabral. (2019). Teach your dog not to jump out of the CAR - Car safety - Dog training video [Video]. *YouTube*. https://www.youtube.com/watch?v=0uYZGPz03Fo

Rodriguez, J. (2012). Sporting group dogs | Common dog training and behavior problems. *Do Behave*. http://www.do-behave.com/ct-dog-trainer/sporting-group-dogs.html

RSPCA. (n.d.-a). How to stop your dog barking too much. *RSCPA*. https://www.rspca.org.uk/adviceandwelfare/pets/dogs/behaviour/barking

RSPCA. (n.d.-b). Train your dog to stop pulling on the lead. *RSPCA*. https://www.rspca.org.uk/adviceandwelfare/pets/dogs/trainin g/walknicely

RSPCA. (2019, September 19). How do I introduce a new dog or puppy to children? *RSPCA*. https://kb.rspca.org.au/knowledge-base/how-do-i-introduce-a-new-dog-or-puppy-to-children/#:~:text=When%20it%20is%20time%20for

Schade, V. (2021, August 9). How to crate train a dog: Step-by-step ionstructions. *BeChewy*. https://be.chewy.com/how-to-crate-train-a-puppy-a-step-by-step-guide-from-an-expert/

Schmidt, E. (2022, October 19). This pet parenting style makes your dog the happiest and most social. *The Dodo*. https://www.thedodo.com/dodowell/want-secure-resilient-dog-parent-way-study-says

Schoniger, S. (2018, December 11). The impact of nutrition on your dog's moods and behavior. *Dog Is Good*. https://www.dogisgood.com/the-impact-of-nutrition-on-your-dogs-moods-and-behavior/#:~:text=If%20your%20dog%20isn

Scott, J. P., & Fuller, J. L. (2012). *Genetics and the social behavior of the dog*. The University of Chicago Press.

Sharpe, S. (2021, November 5). How to crate train your dog in 9 easy steps. *American Kennel Club*. https://www.akc.org/expert-advice/training/how-to-crate-train-your-dog-in-9-easy-steps/

Small Door Veterinary. (n.d.). Everything you need to know about caring for your new dog. *Small Door Veterinary*. https://assets.ctfassets.net/82d3r48zq721/22nWe0saMAC9LY TCfAGdHZ/74d38778d3eb51128bb52734be5339ff/Small-Door-Veterinary-Dog-Parenting-101.pdf

Stregowski, J. (2020, April 23). Adopting a dog? Here's how to prepare for bringing home a new friend. *The Spruce Pets*. https://www.thesprucepets.com/after-adopting-a-dog-1117330

Terrier Rescue. (n.d.). Ten top tips to terriers. *Terrier Rescue*. https://www.terrierrescue.co.uk/ten-top-tips-to-terriers/

The Humane Society Of The United States. (n.d.). How to get your dog to stop barking. *The Humane Society of the United States*. https://www.humanesociety.org/resources/how-get-your-dog-stop-barking#:~:text=Ignore%20the%20barking&text=Regular%20exercise%20and%20the%20use

The Humane Society of the United States. (n.d.). Positive reinforcement training. *The Humane Society of the United States*. https://www.humanesociety.org/resources/positive-reinforcement-training

The Humane Society of the United States. (2018). Crate training 101. *The Humane Society of the United States*. https://www.humanesociety.org/resources/crate-training-101

Todd, Z. (2021, April 14). 13 common dog training mistakes and how to avoid them. *Companion Animal Psychology*. https://www.companionanimalpsychology.com/2021/04/13-common-dog-training-mistakes-and-how.html

Trot, S. (2021, June 4). Helping a rescue dog to overcome trauma: How to build trust. *Now Fresh*. https://nowfresh.com/en/helping-a-rescue-dog-to-overcome-trauma

Trott, S. (2021, May 21). How to train a herding dog. *SpiritDog Training*. https://spiritdogtraining.com/how-to-train-a-herding-dog/

True, C. (2020, June 23). Adopting a rescued dog? Know the signs of trauma. *Healthy Paws*. https://blog.healthypawspetinsurance.com/adopting-a-rescued-pet-watch-for-signs-of-trauma-and-be-patient#:~:text=Dogs%20who%20have%20suffered%20abuse

Truzy, T. (2022, April 12). 8 steps to prepare you for your new rescue dog. *PetHelpful*. https://pethelpful.com/dogs/8-Steps-to-Prepare-you-for-Your-New-Rescue-Dog

Tupler, T. (2020, July 30). How to use a crate for potty training an older dog. *PetMD*. https://www.petmd.com/dog/training/ins-and-outs-potty-training-older-dogs-0

Turner, J. F. (2022, February 6). Tips to train a bull terrier. *Animal Wised*. https://www.animalwised.com/tips-to-train-a-bull-terrier-945.html

Wag Walking. (n.d.). Behavioral problems in dogs - symptoms, causes, diagnosis, treatment, recovery, management, cost. *Wag Walking*. https://wagwalking.com/condition/behavioral-problems

Wiginton, K. (2021, July 15). Prepare your home and family for a dog. *Fetch*. https://pets.webmd.com/dogs/adoption-21/dog-prep-family-home

Wild Earth. (n.d.). Got a yappy dog? How to stop a dog from barking. *Wild Earth*. https://wildearth.com/blogs/dog-knowledge/how-to-stop-a-dog-from-barking

Will Atherton Canine Training. (2021). How to stop your dog PULLING on the leash [Video]. *YouTube*. https://www.youtube.com/watch?v=DU1Kz7NWrWc

Withrow, D. (2018). Why do dogs try to jump on you. *WagWalking*. https://wagwalking.com/behavior/why-do-dogs-try-to-jump-on-you

Yates, J. T. (2021, July 15). 9 things to know before getting a pet. *RACV*. https://www.racv.com.au/royalauto/lifestyle-home/pets/how-to-prepare-home-for-pet.html

Yes, Dog! (n.d.). Force free. *Yes, Dog!* https://yesdog.ca/force-free/

Zak George's Dog Training Revolution. (2015). *How to STOP your dog from running out of the front door! Stay while distracted* [Video]. *YouTube.* https://www.youtube.com/watch?v=6yw_l3Ci_Q0

Zoom Room. (n.d.). How to stop a dog from jumping up in 5 easy steps. *Zoom Room Dog Training.* https://zoomroom.com/admin/stop-dog-jumping/

Image References

825545. (2015, March 16). Walking on lead [Image]. *Pixabay.* https://pixabay.com/photos/dachshund-dog-school-dog-training-672780/

Collingwood, C. C. (2022, May 12). Dog barking [Image]. *Unsplash.* https://unsplash.com/photos/b0nRWZ2P8Tw

Coulton, M. (2020, September 22). Dog playing with toys [Image]. *Pexels.* https://www.pexels.com/photo/a-dog-lying-on-the-floor-4445461/

Gabe. (2022, January 2). Two dogs playing [Image]. *Pexels.* https://www.pexels.com/photo/close-up-shot-of-dogs-playing-together-10705801/

Handa, M. (2017, July 11). Pug jumping [Image]. *Pixabay.* https://pixabay.com/photos/pug-tongue-jumping-dog-2494575/

Hunter, M. (2016, February 27). Sad dog on carpet [Image]. *Unsplash.* https://unsplash.com/photos/iS0Aq3QPsJ4

Street, J. (2018, September 3). Dog reading book [Image]. *Unsplash.* https://unsplash.com/photos/MoDcnVRN5JU

Toshima Style. (2022, December 27). Dog running on grass [Image]. *Pexels.* https://www.pexels.com/photo/a-brown-dog-running-on-brown-grass-14866443/

Verschueren, A. (2021, September 21). Dog in crate [Image]. *Unsplash.* https://unsplash.com/photos/qvbG3-tZnyc

Warrington, B. (2019, May 3). Four dogs sitting together [Image]. *Unsplash.* https://unsplash.com/photos/WSAOGHKEqFc